I call to you, God,
and you answer me.
Listen to me now,
and hear what I say.

PSALM 17:6 NCV

THE 100
MOST IMPORTANT
BIBLE VERSES
FOR teens

Presented to:

_____

Presented by:

_____

Date:

_____

Make me walk in the path of Your commandments, for I delight in it.

PSALM 119:35 NKJV

THE 100
MOST IMPORTANT
BIBLE VERSES
FOR teens

W PUBLISHING GROUP
A Division of Thomas Nelson Publishers
Since 1798
www.wpublishinggroup.com

The 100 Most Important Bible Verses for Teens
©2005 by GRQ, Inc.
Brentwood, Tennessee 37027

Published by W Publishing Group, a Division of Thomas Nelson, Inc., P.O. Box 141000, Nashville, Tennessee 37214.

W Publishing Group books may be purchased in bulk for educational, business, fundraising, or sales promotional use. For information, please email SpecialMarkets@ThomasNelson.com.

Scripture quotations are from the following sources:

• The New Century Version® (NCV). Copyright © 1987, 1988, 1991 by Word Publishing, a Division of Thomas Nelson, Inc. Used by permission. All rights reserved. • The New King James Version® (NKJV), copyright © 1979, 1980, 1982, Thomas Nelson, Inc., Publishers. • The Contemporary English Version (CEV) © 1991 by the American Bible Society. Used by permission. • God's Word (GOD'S WORD) is a copyrighted work of God's Word to the Nations Bible Society. Quotations are used by permission. Copyright 1995 by God's Word to the Nations Bible Society. All rights reserved. • Good News Translation, Second Edition (GNT), copyright © 1992 by American Bible Society. Used by permission. All rights reserved. • New Living Translation (NLT), copyright © 1996 by Tyndale House Publishers, Inc., Wheaton, Ill. All rights reserved. • The Message (MSG), copyright ©1993. Used by permission of NavPress Publishing Group. • New American Standard Bible (NASB), © 1960, 1977, 1995 by the Lockman Foundation.

Managing Editor: Lila Empson
Associate Editor: Laura Kendall
Manuscript: Robi Lipscomb and J. Heyward Rogers
Design: Thatcher Design, Nashville, Tennessee

Library of Congress Cataloging-in-Publication Data
100 most important Bible verses for teens
  p. cm.
ISBN 0-8499-0030-1
1. Teenagers—religious life. 2. Bible—Quotations I. Title: One hundred most important Bible verses for teens. II. W. Publishing Group

BV4531.3.A15 2005
220.5′2—dc22

                    2005010206

Printed in China
05 06 07 08 — 9 8 7 6 5 4 3 2 1

Do not change yourselves to be like the people of this world, but be changed within by a new way of thinking. Then you will be able to decide what God wants for you; you will know what is good and pleasing to him and what is perfect.

ROMANS 12:2 NCV

Contents

Seek the LORD while He may be found,
call upon Him while He is near.

ISAIAH 55:6 NKJV

Introduction

With each word in the Bible, God whispers, "I love you." The people in the Bible are just like you in more ways than you can imagine. Recorded in the one hundred verses chosen for this book are messages from God to you. They will guide you, comfort you, excite you, teach you, and encourage you. They will entice you to read more verses in the Bible. If you do that, it will change your life because you will read the words that God has just for your life.

No one Scripture is most important or better than the rest. Each one joins the others to form an awesome picture of God's plan for your life. Though the words have been around for a long time, they have surprising relevance for your life.

The one hundred verses selected for their importance to you as a teen are drawn from an exciting array of Old and New Testament books. God spoke through earthshaking and ordinary events, and through prophets and ordinary people to bring insights and truth that are timelessly right-on. These Bible verses contain information on friendships, dating, sex, parents, purity, your future, and more.

Some verses will challenge you to think. A few will change the way you think. One or two may change your life. The Bible is one place you are sure to find God. Ask God right now to do all these things and more as you dig into the Bible and discover how these one hundred verses fit into your life.

In the beginning God created the heavens and the earth.

GENESIS 1:1 NKJV

In the Beginning God Thought of You

Don't you wish you could have been there when God created the world? The process of designing the moon, the sun, and the planets must have been incredible. The power and creativity give you just a glimpse of God and all he is capable of. Creating heaven and earth involved science, math, biology, chemistry, and all sorts of other school subjects that humans wouldn't begin to discover until years after the creation event.

Much of creation remains a mystery today. A lot of what God does is just too huge for the human mind to comprehend. The creation of the heavens and the earth is a loud statement from God to you about who he is, how powerful he is, and what his plan is. God used his power to arrange the intimate

> **If God can create a star out of nothing, imagine what he can do with your life.**

details of the world you live in. God didn't make just one tree for you; he made hundreds of thousands of species of trees.

God's power created all you need to live including water, food, and shelter. His abilities go beyond supplying your physical needs, however; he supplies direction for a great life. It is no small thing to create even one star. If God can create a star out of nothing, imagine what he can do with your life. It is comforting to know that even in the beginning God took a personal interest in you and provided exactly what you need to live.

God designed the world with you in mind. Look around and enjoy the details of life that God made for you to enjoy. Look for God in the details around you.

The LORD is good, a stronghold in the day of trouble; and He knows those who trust in Him.

NAHUM 1:7 NKJV

God Protects You

The people of Nineveh had messed up once before, and a hundred years later they were again choosing to live their own way. By indulging their desires, they had removed themselves from the safety and protection of God. Getting your way has a certain appeal in the beginning because it seems to offer freedom, fun, sensuality, and excitement. The appeal, however, is lost once you realize your way may not be as good as God's way for your life. His way for your life includes boundaries, but they are designed to ensure your safety.

Choosing to live according to God's will is like choosing a safe shelter for your life. The Hebrew word for *stronghold* used in Nahum 1:7 is *ma'owz*, which means "a place of safety, protection, refuge." Imagine two houses. One house is more like a castle with a moat, tall solid walls, and thick wooden doors designed to keep anyone inside safe from harm. The other house has standard doors, walls, and windows. Living in God's will is like living in a castle, compared to living in a regular house.

> God will be there for you when pain, disappointment, and frustration threaten to invade your life.

The people of Nineveh drifted back into the habit of doing things their way and ignoring God. As a result of ditching God's ways, they left themselves unprotected and open to attack from their enemies. Speaking through Nahum, God called them back to the protection of his will. God will be there for you when pain, disappointment, and frustration threaten to invade your life. When you feel like you are under attack, whether at home, at school, or at work, God offers you his protection. Nahum's message was this: God is good. Living within God's loving will puts you in the most secure position you can be.

If you choose to live outside God's boundaries, in a sense you're choosing also to live outside his protection. What areas of your life need to be brought within the walls of God's stronghold?

I can do all things through Christ who strengthens me.

PHILIPPIANS 4:13 NKJV

You Can Do It

With open wounds from recent beatings, Paul wrote his fellow believers from prison. While thanking them for their prayers, he assured them that he would be all right. By depending on the strength of God rather than on his own strength, Paul knew he would be okay.

After surviving a shipwreck and starting a fire to warm himself, a poisonous snake jumped from the wood and bit Paul. Paul was miraculously unaffected by the bite. In one of the prisons Paul was confined to, the walls fell down, the chains around Paul's legs fell off, and he was freed.

According to another letter written by Paul, he was beaten repeatedly, almost stoned to death, and shipwrecked three times, risking his life constantly to teach about Jesus. Paul was a strong person who acknowledged that his strength came from God.

You may be facing circumstances beyond your control. Maybe there is something you want to do, but you can't imagine doing it on your own. It's vital for you to realize that you can allow God to be your strength. Tell God when you feel

> **It's vital for you to realize that you can allow God to be your strength.**

weak, and talk to him about your dreams. Remember Paul's story if you are struggling to overcome an addiction, suffering the pain of a relationship that ended badly, or just trying to get through another long day. Ask God to provide the strength to survive the shipwrecks in your life. With God's help, Paul went from being a persecutor of Christians to one of the greatest heroes of the faith. With God, you can do anything.

God offers his greatness so you can live a life with endless possibilities. Allow your mind to explore all the things you could do by relying on the strength of God.

Seek the LORD while He may be found;
call upon Him while He is near.

ISAIAH 55:6 NKJV

Find God

You're young. You probably have a lot of life ahead of you. So when is a good time to get serious about seeking God? There's no better time than the present. "Seek the LORD while He may be found," said Isaiah. There's an urgency to that message. God is findable. Seek him. Don't let him get away—or, rather, don't let your life get away from you. The habits you establish now will be hard to break later. Get into the habit of seeking God now; if you don't—if you get settled into habits that don't include

God—he might not be so easy to find later.

Make it a habit to seek God in your daily activities. Seek God when you wake; seek God when you study or play or work. Seek God when you're with your friends and when you're among strangers.

At a conference, camp, or retreat God seems to be everywhere. At home afterward, when you dig into the busyness of everyday life, it may seem as if God is hard to find. This verse reminds you that God is near and that you can always find him.

It is important for you to know that God is near and will never leave you. God is near you at school and at home. God is near you even though no one else can see or no one else is looking. God is near when your friends are there for you and when your friends are gone. God is near you by the lockers and alongside the gossipers. God is everywhere, no matter where you are.

> God is near you even though no one else can see or no one else is looking.

How can you find God right here, right now? It is easy. God is near you this very minute. You will find God when you pray or talk to God.

> God created human beings in his image. In the image of God he created them. He created them male and female.

GENESIS 1:27 NCV

You Have the Look

Clear skin. A perfect body. The right clothes. If you're like most teens, you spend a lot of time thinking about your appearance. It's no mystery why. Your peers have a habit of judging one another by appearances. On top of that, the media seem determined to convince you that your looks are the most important part of who you are. Think how many of the ads on TV are for things that are supposed to make you look better. TV shows are full of beautiful people. Magazine covers feature the hottest-looking guys or girls.

It may be hard to believe sometimes, but ultimately it doesn't much matter what other people think about the way you look. You are made in the image of God. You are patterned after the Creator of the universe, but not in the way you look. After all, you can't see God. It is your inner self that reflects God's image—your character, your creativity, your capacity for love.

> It may be hard to believe sometimes, but ultimately it doesn't much matter what other people think about the way you look.

Make it a habit to correct your "vision" when you check your image. Learn to see God in you. (He's there!) Learn to see what God loves about you.

When you look in a mirror, the image you see reflected there isn't the real you—certainly not the whole you. The most important reflection is not the one you see in the mirror; the most important is the reflection of God's image in your life. You have a lot to show the world: your heart and soul reflect the God of the universe. That's an image you can be proud of.

You are more than what you see in the mirror. If you really want to make an impression on people, show them what you've got inside.

God will wipe away every tear from their eyes, and there will be no more death, sadness, crying, or pain, because all the old ways are gone.

No More Tears

Chapter 21 in the book of Revelation is a visual and emotional masterpiece describing heaven. There are layers of precious stones including sapphire, emerald, topaz and more that form the foundation of the city. The city walls are pure gold. The streets are pure gold so polished that they appear to look like glass. There will be light everywhere. The light will come from God himself. The most incredible part of heaven may not be what you see; it may be what is missing that most demands your attention.

22   THE 100 MOST IMPORTANT BIBLE VERSES FOR TEENS

In heaven you will not find sin, Satan, or death. Anything in your present life that causes you pain, sadness, or even difficulty will vanish. Ignorance and misunderstanding will give way to complete understanding. Fear will be replaced by peace. Complete healing will occur, restoring every person. Nothing will wear out or decay; everything will be made whole and perfect. There will be no more good-byes. Best of all, death,

> It is a great comfort to know there will be a time and a place where the worst of your present circumstances will be gone.

both natural and violent, will cease to exist. Tears will no longer be needed.

It is a great comfort to know there will be a time and a place where the worst of your present circumstances will be gone. For you, all the questions will be answered, and your faith will be complete. He will touch your face, wipe your tears, and welcome you to a joyful eternity.

Happy endings are not just a fairy tale. Ending up with God guarantees that you will live happily ever after and eternally with the One who loves you the most.

The LORD is with me like a strong warrior, so those who are chasing me will trip and fall; they will not defeat me.

JEREMIAH 20:11 NCV

He Will Defend You

Do you ever feel picked on—like someone is out to hurt you? Maybe a teacher has it in for you. Maybe a gossip is spreading lies about you. Maybe a bully has chosen you for a target.

Jeremiah knew a thing or two about that. The powers that be in his society didn't appreciate his style of truth-telling, and he found himself on their bad side. In fact, they threw him in an empty cistern—a big, dark underground tank for storing rainwater—and left him there to die (until a friend came to rescue him). Another time he was thrown into the stocks for public humiliation. That's when Jeremiah spoke the words "The LORD is with me like a strong warrior, so those who are chasing me will trip and fall."

God was Jeremiah's defender, in spite of the trouble Jeremiah found himself in. God is your defender too, your strong warrior. It is good to know that God is your bodyguard, not so much in a physical sense, but more in the sense of helping you know how to handle tough situations. As you rely on God to protect you when you are hurting, he will direct and strengthen

> **As you rely on God to protect you when you are hurting, he will direct and strengthen you to get through any situation.**

you to get through any situation. Your enemies will trip and fall while you stand firm. It may not be today, but you can trust in God's justice.

Lay your troubles before God, and see how he delivers you.

*L*ove your enemies, bless those who curse you, do good to those who hate you, and pray for those who spitefully use you and persecute you.

MATTHEW 5:44 NKJV

Love Your Enemies

There's nothing more earsplitting than the feedback you get from a microphone held too close to a speaker. The speaker amplifies any sound picked up by the mike. The mike picks up the amplified sound and sends it back through the speaker, where it is amplified again and sent back through the loop, and in a matter of a couple of seconds, you've got a noise so shrill and loud that nobody can stand to be in the room.

The hatred of two enemies is like that. Enemy A picks up the meanness of Enemy B and sends it back a little louder and a little shriller. Enemy B gets the new, exaggerated meanness from Enemy A and sends it back with even greater force. The loop of hatred quickly produces something so loud and shrill that no one wants to be around the two combatants.

> **When Jesus instructed his followers to love their enemies, he was teaching them to break the feedback loop of hatred.**

But a feedback loop is easy enough to correct. You just turn off the mike or hold it farther away from the speaker so it can't feed back the noise. The loop is broken. Everything falls silent. And the relief of everyone in the room is so great you can almost touch it.

When Jesus instructed his followers to love their enemies, he was teaching them to break the feedback loop of hatred. When you do good to those who hate you, when you pray for those who treat you badly, you break the cycle of hatred and meanness, and peace prevails.

Who are your enemies? Pray for them right now. Do something good for them. You can break the feedback loop of hatred.

LORD, I have heard the news about you; I am amazed at what you have done. LORD, do great things once again in our time; make those things happen again in our own days. Even when you are angry, remember to be kind.

HABAKKUK 3:2 NCV

God Will Amaze You

God has a pretty amazing reputation. Habakkuk had heard stories about how God had rescued his people from terrible trouble. Based on God's reputation, Habakkuk boldly asked God to do it again. In Habakkuk's prayer, recorded in chapter 3 verses 2–18, he recalled some of the incredible things God had done over time. By recounting the fantastic ways God had rescued his people in the past,

Habakkuk reassured himself that God would rescue his people again. Habakkuk recalled how in the past God caused an ocean to separate so God's people could walk safely across to the other side and avoid being captured by their enemies. Habakkuk prayed that God would do something of that magnitude to rescue the people of his time.

> God is an endless source of amazement. Be bold like Habakkuk and ask God to do for your generation what he has done in the past.

You can read about God's reputation throughout the Bible. It is a story that continues today because God continues to do amazing things. God listens to your prayers at any time of the day or night. He inspires people to write and record music for you to listen to. He causes the sun to rise and start each new day. God is an endless source of amazement. Be bold like Habakkuk and ask God to do for your generation what he has done in the past. Based on his reputation, you will not be disappointed with his response.

Write down a few of the fabulous ways you have been thrilled by God. Keep the list handy as a source of encouragement.

All those who stand before others and say they believe in me, I, the Son of Man, will say before the angels of God that they belong to me.

LUKE 12:8 NCV

Stand Up for Jesus

Jesus vigorously addressed hypocrisy—saying one thing and doing the opposite. Even the twelve disciples, who knew Jesus personally and walked with him every day for three years, fought with their own hypocrisy. It was difficult to say they believed that Jesus was the King, the Savior whom the Bible predicted. They risked imprisonment or death for what they believed. Jesus understood the danger they faced; he even knew they would deny knowing him at times. But he still expected them to love him and believe in him enough to fearlessly acknowledge and proclaim him as the Savior.

Jesus invested three years of his life teaching and training the disciples, knowing that after he was gone they would be the ones who continued to spread the word about God. He knew they would risk embarrassment, harassment, and even death to tell other people about his love and about his plan for every person. They

> You are precious to God and he is watching over all you do, including the times you stand up for what you believe in.

needed to know how central they were to the survival of the truth about God.

You are precious to God and he is watching over all you do, including the times you stand up for what you believe in. God will watch over you when you step out of your comfort zone to tell others about God. As you talk about what you believe, you are continuing what the disciples bravely started.

Your voice raised in praise of who God is will be heard here on earth and in heaven. Shout out what you believe. Your words count.

Give freely to the poor person, and do not wish that you didn't have to give. The LORD your God will bless your work and everything you touch.

DEUTERONOMY 15:10 NCV

It Is Good to Give

If you've ever lifted weights, you understand the saying "No pain, no gain." You build muscle mass by pushing your muscles beyond what they can now do. Actually, you're making tiny tears in the muscle that are filled in with more muscle. And that hurts. Your ability to give grows in much the same way. When you give a little more than you thought you could—when you give till it hurts—God always fills in the gaps, bulks you up. And as you get stronger, it gets easier to do the heavy lifting that generosity requires.

You can give in different ways. You can give peace to your family by being ready on time to go on a family outing. You can give time to your church by helping out in the nursery. You can give comfort to your friends

> **When you give sacrificially, you put yourself in a position to watch God do amazing things.**

by listening to them. You can give support to someone in need by praying for that person. You can give pride to your community by picking up trash.

When you give more than you thought you could, you have to rely on the power of God to provide what you don't have. God always comes through, even if it's not in the same way you were expecting. When you give sacrificially, you put yourself in a position to watch God do amazing things. What better way to grow into a spiritual heavyweight yourself?

The more you give to God, the more blessings you receive. You can't outgive God, but it might be interesting and fun to try.

These things did not really come from me and my people. Everything comes from you; we have given you back what you gave us.

1 CHRONICLES 29:14 NCV

It All Belongs to God

"Mom, can I have five dollars?" The five-year-old boy looks expectantly into his mother's eyes. "What do you need with five dollars?" she asks. "I want to buy you a present." The mother, when she receives her son's five-dollar present, won't be five dollars ahead of the game. But that's not the point anyway. Her son's gift is an expression of his love for her. It's his way of saying he would love to shower her with gifts if only he could. That gesture does more to strengthen their relationship than any other exchange of goods and money could.

Any gift you offer up puts you in the position of that five-year-old boy. You can't give God anything that isn't his already. When you offer up your talents for God's service, you've giving back talents that came from God. When you drop money in the offering plate, that's money God gave you first. And that's a wonderful expression of love for God.

> **You can't give God anything that isn't his already.**

The point isn't that you're helping God out. The point is that you're acknowledging that everything is his; by giving a portion of it back to him, you begin to appreciate even more the portion that he freely gives you to use. That expression of love is what pleases God and builds your relationship with him—not because you've met his needs, but because you have come to him like a child offering a gift of thanks to a loving Father.

It all belongs to God. God has given you all that you need to give to others; besides, you can't out give God.

Give freely to the poor person, and do not wish that you didn't have to give. The Lord your God will bless your work and everything you touch.

DEUTERONOMY 15:10 NCV

To all who did accept him and believe in him he gave the right to become children of God.

JOHN 1:12 NCV

Become a Child of God

Christian music artist Geoff Moore will tell you that the moment he held Anna Grace in his arms, he had the clearest picture of what it meant to be a child of God. Geoff and his wife, Jan, traveled across miles and over oceans to claim their adopted daughter from an orphanage in China. To this day Geoff is moved with emotion when he describes how he was overwhelmed with love for this little girl whom he knew nothing about. It did not matter to him where she came from or where she was found. He is her father, and she is his child. That's the way it is with adoption. The child is deliberately chosen. Adoption is no accident or something that just happens. Adoption is an act of compassion and fulfillment and love.

God loves you more than you can imagine. Adoption is a picture of God's love for you. Your adoption is a new birth. You are not born again physically; you are born spiritually into God's family. You are his child, and he is your good Father.

> **Adoption is a picture of God's love for you. Your adoption is a new birth.**

In addition to his everlasting, abundant love, he provides guidance and protection.

God accepts you as his child just the way you are. Just as Anna Grace did nothing to earn Geoff's and Jan's love, you don't need to do anything to earn God's love. Where you come from does not matter to him. What matters is that you reach out for him. He simply takes you into his arms and claims you as his child once and for all time.

Reach out to God with the heart of a child. He will welcome and love you as his very own.

The LORD spoke his word to me, "Before I formed you in the womb, I knew you. Before you were born, I set you apart for my holy purpose."

JEREMIAH 1:4–5 GOD'S WORD

God Already Knew

"Nobody understands me." It's the universal cry of the teenager. You're not always sure you understand yourself, and you're sure your parents and teachers, maybe even your friends, don't understand where you're coming from. But God knows you. He made you, and he made you for a purpose. Even if you feel confused and misunderstood, God never loses sight of what he made you for.

God knew what color your eyes would be, what your favorite food would be, and who you would grow up to be even before your mom and dad met. God chose your family and your birthday and your purpose. God loves you just the way you are. You are unique and important to him. You are the one

> **You are the one person who can do what God designed you to do.**

person who can do what God designed you to do. Nothing about you is a surprise to God. You are useful and valuable to God.

As you seek God and serve him, you will begin to understand his purpose for your life. It won't be clear all at one time; God probably won't speak to you with a booming voice from the heavens or shine a brilliant light on your forehead. But isn't it good to know that you were set apart for some holy purpose before you were ever born? God knows the plans he has for you.

In God's eyes no one can take your place. You are the perfect one-of-a-kind combination of qualities and characteristics that he created.

D̶o not spread false rumors, and do not help a guilty person by giving false testimony.

EXODUS 23:1 GNT

Be Honest

If you've ever been the subject of a rumor at school, you know how a rumor can take on a life of its own. It races around the cafeteria and down the hallways like a lit fuse racing toward a stick of dynamite at the other end. Who knows what kind of damage it'll cause when the whole thing blows? Even the person who started the rumor—whether intentionally or unintentionally—has no control over it once it gets started.

When you spread a rumor, you are actually helping someone else hurt another person. You get yourself involved in someone else's guilt. Sure, it's hard to keep a juicy tidbit to yourself. But when you do resist the temptation to gossip—even more, when you refuse to believe bad things about another person without hard evidence—you make a big difference in the atmosphere around you. You are suddenly part of the solution rather than the problem.

God established laws that strengthen families, friends, and communities. At the heart of all good relationships is a trust built on honesty. Lies and rumors destroy trust and ignite all kinds of bad feelings like anger, revenge, and hate. Rumors and lies erode the foundation of honesty. God's laws are designed to ensure that people treat one another with fairness

> When you spread a rumor, you are actually helping someone else hurt another person.

and honesty. Life is a lot easier when your parents and friends and teachers trust you. If you want to inspire that kind of trust, make honesty your goal at all times.

The next time you hear a hurtful rumor, take a stand: believe the best about others unless there's clear evidence that you shouldn't. You might be surprised at the impact you can have by refusing to pass along a rumor.

As pressure and stress bear down on me,
I find joy in your commands.

PSALM 119:143 NLT

From Stress to Joy

When the pressure and stress of life are building, joy is a welcome find. The pressure to fit in and the stress of grades and homework can get anyone down. Few people like to be told what to do, and yet when God asks you to do something, it's different. It's different because God asks you to do the things that will make your life easier and more enjoyable in the long run. His requests are based on his deep love and true concern for your life.

When Jesus was asked what the greatest commandment was, he replied that people should first love God and then love others. A practical example of how God's commands can bring you joy is found as you focus each day on loving God and loving others. Something happens when you turn the focus away from yourself. By

> **God's commands are a guide to living a fabulous life.**

turning the focus on others, you spend less time stressing about yourself. Plus, it feels good to love other people.

God's instructions are a loving plan for a successful, enjoyable life. God knows the challenges you face. God asks you to love others as you would love yourself. He asks you to be honest and respectful. God wants you to put him first in your life. By following his directions, you will avoid and eliminate problems and confusion in your life. God's commands are a guide to living a fabulous life.

Living in your own strength is a good way to get worn down. Embrace God's plan for your life, and live in the joy it brings.

Jesus sat down and called the twelve apostles to him. He said, "Whoever wants to be the most important must be last of all and servant of all."

MARK 9:35 NCV

If You Want to Be First, Be Last

The disciples, the followers closest to Jesus, got caught arguing about which one of them was the greatest. Jesus had frequently shown them that following God wasn't about being great or first; it was about serving others and putting the needs of others first. To be great in God's kingdom, you have to put other people first and yourself last.

Putting others first is more than the occasional random act of kindness where you do something nice for someone. It is living your life with other people's needs first, not just sometime, but all the time. At home you might offer to fix a meal for your family, or you could consider your family's schedule first before making your own plans. At school you could invite someone who normally sits alone to sit with you and your friends. Putting others first involves listening and hearing what they really need. Putting others first requires treating everyone equally regardless of their status, their past, or popular opinion. In addition to putting

> **Putting others first requires treating everyone equally regardless of their status, their past, or popular opinion.**

others first, you can go a step further by serving others too.

By putting others first, you will be in a position to serve others. Make it your goal to serve instead of being served. God's love comes alive for other people when you serve them. You become a living example of God's love. As you selflessly serve others, you will become the kind of great person that Jesus was hoping for in his disciples. You will be a great servant of others.

If you put others first, logically speaking you will be last. Get at the end of the line and see what needs to be done for the people in front of you.

> God began doing a good work in you,
> and I am sure he will continue it until it is
> finished when Jesus Christ comes again.

PHILIPPIANS 1:6 NCV

God's Project

You've done it again. You've fallen into that old habit, committed that pet sin one more time. After confessing it a hundred times, promising yourself and God you'd never do it again, here you are. Same song, hundred and first verse. You're ready to tattoo a big *L* on your forehead: it's looking like you're going to be a loser forever.

But if you're in Christ, that's not who the Bible says you are. The Bible says you're headed for perfection. God has begun a good work in you, and he will see it through to the end. When God looks at you, he sees the finished product he's making out of you. Of course it's discouraging to commit the same old sins you've tried to overcome before. But don't give up. Because as you work to be more like God, it's really God who is at work in you. Each time you mess up, just promise yourself that you'll keep trying, because one of these days you're going to succeed with God's help.

When you've messed up, it's natural to think that your low self-image reflects what God must think about you. You need to learn instead to let God's opinion of you shape your self-image. He is perfecting you; he's not finished yet, but he

> When God looks at you, he sees the finished product he's making out of you.

thinks you're worth the trouble. That's not to say that you shouldn't be bothered by your sins. The conscience that speaks up when you've done wrong comes from God. Let that bad feeling turn you back to God and a new start. Don't let it turn you inward, to self-pity, discouragement, and defeat. God will finish what he's started.

What are the pet sins and bad habits that make you feel like a loser? Give them to God once again.

GOD told Samuel, "Looks aren't everything. Don't be impressed with his looks and stature. I've already eliminated him. GOD judges persons differently than humans do. Men and women look at the face; GOD looks into the heart."

1 SAMUEL 16:7 MSG

Not Just Looks

Jock. Geek. Queen bee. Stoner. Snob. If you can figure out what category to stick a person in, that's all you need to know. Or is it? Categories don't tell you anything about what's inside a person. And yet that's who a person really is. Heart, character, soul—they're all on the inside. The inside is what God sees when he looks at a person.

When the prophet Samuel went to Jesse's house looking for the next king of Israel, he put young David in the same categories that David's family put him in: the little brother, the shepherd boy, certainly no king. But God told Samuel to look again. In David's heart, God saw the man who would lead his people to greatness.

> When you put people in a category, you've written them off, as if you've got them all figured out.

Sure, it's hard—maybe impossible—to see what's inside another person. But that's the point. When you put people in a category, you've written them off, as if you've got them all figured out: she fits in Category X, so I know she's going to do this, believe that, and feel that other thing. But people are never that simple. On the inside, they're just as complicated as you are.

So be careful when you dismiss another person with a flippant "I know his type." Samuel and Jesse and David's brothers thought they knew David's type, but he was one in a million. So are you. So is everybody you've ever known.

Pick one of the social groups at your school—one of the groups that you think you "know their type." Commit to get to know at least one of those people as an individual.

> Whoever compels you to go one mile, go with him two.

MATTHEW 5:41 NKJV

The Extra Mile

You know the drill: "If everyone just does his or her part, we'll be finished in no time." Okay. But you can pretty much be sure not everybody's going to do his or her part. "Leave the campsite as clean as you found it." Fine. But somebody out there is going to leave it dirtier than they found it. The point is, unless there are at least some people who are willing to do their share, the people who don't do their fair share are going to end up messing things up for everybody else. The job won't get done. The campsite will become a junk pile.

The same is true of your relationships. In theory, if everyone would just meet in the middle, everyone would get along great. But unfortunately, not everyone gets all the way to the middle. It may be because that person is hardheaded, or maybe he or she has a legitimate difference of opinion about where the middle is. Either way, if you go only to the middle and no further, there's going to be a gap in the relationship. You may feel you've done your share, but the relationship is still broken.

> **You keep your relationships healthy not by meeting in the middle, but by going the extra mile.**

You keep your relationships healthy not by meeting in the middle, but by going the extra mile. That way, even if you and another person disagree about the exact location of the middle, you have plenty of margin for error. You can still meet, even if it's not exactly in the middle.

Don't be one of those people who spend more effort arguing about whose job it is than they would have spent just picking up the other person's slack. Sometimes going the extra mile is easier than haggling over what's your fair share.

"I say this because I know what I am planning for you," says the LORD. "I have good plans for you, not plans to hurt you. I will give you hope and a good future."

JEREMIAH 29:11 NCV

The Good Life

God is in control of the future—your future in particular. God has your future planned. God knows everything you will do. God has a plan for you that he won't give up on.

The prophet Jeremiah wrote a letter to a group of people who believed in God but who were exiles in a country far from their home. The letter contained good news and bad news. God promised he had a good plan for their lives; however, they would first have to endure the consequences of not obeying God. God wanted them to know that everything they experienced was in his control and part of his plan.

There is no limit to the possibilities in your life when you commit your choices, your heart, and your life to God. Dream big and take your dreams to God. With his unlimited power and resources, nothing is impossible. Your part in his plan is to believe in God and obey him. Believe God can do anything, and never give up hope. You will be amazed at how much God can do in your life. God has a plan for where you will go to school, whom you will

> There is no limit to the possibilities in your life when you commit your choices, your heart, and your life to God.

marry, and what kind of job you will have. Not only does God have knowledge of your future mate and career, but he also knows what you need to do. Your future will be more than you hoped for with him involved. Isn't it a comfort to know that your future rests not on your own abilities, but on God's?

Your future is in God's hands. What are you hoping for? Share your hopes with God and prepare to be amazed, because he has more in mind for you than you can imagine.

EPHESIANS 4:32 NCV

Forgive Because He Forgave You

Paul challenged believers to treat one another as God treated them. Whether people deserve it or not, they should be treated with kindness. If God can love and forgive you, then you, too, can love and forgive others.

Jesus lived out this principle. Zacchaeus overcharged people on their taxes and kept the profits for himself. No one liked that dishonest, greedy man, but Jesus went to his home and shared a meal with him. As a result of that small kindness, Zacchaeus changed his ways and dedicated himself to living more like Jesus. On another occasion, Jesus shared a conversation with a woman at a well. He asked her for a drink of water. This woman had a bad reputation. Their conversation inspired her to change her life and share all Jesus told her with the people in her village. As a result, not only was her life changed, but the people of her village believed in Jesus too. Jesus accepted the most unacceptable people. No matter what a person did or was, Jesus offered forgiveness and the opportunity to live a new life.

> There is nothing that gets a person's attention more quickly than showing undeserved kindness to him.

There is nothing that gets a person's attention more quickly than showing undeserved kindness to him. At school or work there might be someone who has hurt you or who is regarded as unacceptable. The kindness and forgiveness Jesus offered to you changed your life. By extending forgiveness to others, you can help change lives too.

If you find it hard to forgive other people, remember what God has forgiven you.

Always remember what is written in the Book of the Teachings. Study it day and night to be sure to obey everything that is written there. If you do this, you will be wise and successful in everything.

JOSHUA 1:8 NCV

More Than Words

Following the rules can be hard for a teen. You feel you're ready to be independent and do things your own way, but your parents and teachers and bosses are still trying to control you with rules that can seem arbitrary or unfair.

Sure, some rules really are arbitrary or unfair. But most rules exist for a good reason. Take the rules of the road.

They are limiting. They don't let you drive on the left side of the road or on the sidewalk. But if you keep within the few limits of the law, you have the freedom to drive wherever you want to. The laws are there to protect everyone's freedom, not to take it away.

The same is true of God's laws. They don't exist to spoil your fun, but to ensure that you succeed. That's why God told Joshua to study his teaching day and night and to obey it—so he would be wise and success-ful. God wants the same thing for you. Within God's guidelines there is tremendous freedom to live a happy and fulfilling life. Step outside those guidelines, and you might run into a head-on collision.

> **Within God's guidelines there is tremendous freedom to live a happy and fulfilling life.**

It's human nature to question the rules. Every now and then, it might even be appropriate to speak up and challenge human rules that seem unfair or not well thought out. But you can be sure that God's rules exist to lead you on to greater happiness. God's laws are just part of his love for you.

~𝑀𝑀○

God's laws are more than simply rules to memorize; God's laws are the way he cares for you. Allow God to show you how much he loves you by reading his laws in the Bible.

Remember that I commanded you to be strong and brave. Don't be afraid, because the LORD your God will be with you everywhere you go.

JOSHUA 1:9 NCV

Be Strong

What are you afraid of? Your world can be a scary place. Hardly a month goes by without a report of violence at a school somewhere. And even if you feel physically safe at school, there are other fears that teens face every day—fear of rejection, fear of failure, fear of a future bearing down with new and strange experiences and challenges.

When God told Joshua to be brave, he didn't say, "You have nothing to fear." No, there is plenty to fear. What he told Joshua was that he would be with him wherever he should go. God's presence makes you brave and gives you strength to face whatever fears life sends your way. If God is for you, who can stand against you?

Notice also that God *commands* bravery and strength. That seems strange in a way. How can you command a person to feel something? Either you feel brave or you don't feel brave, right? But the bravery that God commands is more than a feeling. It's faith. God commands Joshua—and you—to be brave because bravery is evidence that a person believes that God will do

> To wallow in fear is to say that you trust your own feelings more than you trust the God who has promised to take care of you.

what he has said he would do. To wallow in fear is to say that you trust your own feelings more than you trust the God who has promised to take care of you. So be courageous. That's an order.

Remember the times that God has seen you through. God's faithfulness is the basis of your courage.

I trust in God. I will not be afraid. What can people do to me?

PSALM 56:11 NCV

You are tempted in the same way that everyone else is tempted. But God can be trusted not to let you be tempted too much, and he will show you how to escape from your temptations.

1 CORINTHIANS 10:13 CEV

There Is a Way Out

By modeling your life after Jesus and following God's ways, you will have options when temptation comes your way. God doesn't tempt people, but temptation is a part of life. The Bible has story after story about real people who faced real temptation. Some of their stories are examples of mistakes others have made. As you read their stories, you will be helped to avoid the mistakes they made. Many of their stories outline plans for successfully avoiding temptation. Their stories will give you practical advice, encouragement, and wisdom to face temptation and win.

Your best defense against temptation is to run from it. The story of Joseph is a great example. When Potiphar's wife tempted Joseph with sexual advances, he literally ran right out of his jacket to get away from her. God provides you with wisdom and a sense of right and wrong. By leaning on the laws or commandments found

> **Your best defense against temptation is to run from it.**

in the Bible, you will be equipped to recognize temptation when it comes your way. Recognizing temptation is one way you can avoid temptation.

By hanging out with other people who love God, you will be better prepared to fight temptation. Good friends will hold you accountable and will support you as you live a life that is pleasing to God. True friends can pray with you and for you. Friends are another way God helps you face temptations. Temptation may come your way, but God provides the people, the knowledge, and the way out.

When you're in a place where you're being tempted, the way out of temptation is often literally the way out of the place where you're being tempted. Get up and walk out. Nothing says you have to sit there and take it.

If someone obeys God's teaching, then in that person God's love has truly reached its goal.

1 JOHN 2:5 NCV

You Know You Belong

When you fall in love, no one has to tell you to talk to that person every day. You do it to be near that person and to be a part of that person's life. The person you are in love with doesn't have to tell you what to do to please him or her. You make it your mission to know what pleases the person you love, and you do it. Doing things the way your boyfriend or girlfriend wants is not a chore, it's a joy. In a similar way, your response to God's love leads to obedience.

It isn't forced. Obedience is your voluntary surrender to the goodness of God's ways.

The irony of obedience is that the more you know about God, the more you are motivated to make sure that nothing separates you from him. His ways represent the best life has to offer you.

Be sure that you have turned control of your life over to God. John said that your willingness to comply with the laws and the guidance God provides for your life is evidence of your love for God. If your obedience is a result of your own ability to follow rules, you have missed out on what God intended. As you fall in love with God, his laws and direction will cease

> **Obedience is your voluntary surrender to the goodness of God's ways.**

to be rules and will become a gift of love. Your complete surrender to him is your assurance that his love is being made perfect in you.

Answer honestly: Do you work harder at pleasing yourself or pleasing God? Your obedience is evidence of what really matters to you.

The tongue is a small part of the body, but it brags about great things. A big forest fire can be started with only a little flame.

JAMES 3:5 NCV

The Power of Words

One sentence, even one word, has the power to heal or hurt. Imagine walking through the school parking lot and overhearing your name. Though you keep walking, your ears tune in, hoping to hear a kind word, but there is also a concern that you are about to be slammed. Sometimes school seems like a soap opera that plays out with exaggerated words, lies, and half-truths.

James gave an account of how powerful words could be. He used three analogies to make his point. Most horses weigh from eight hundred to one thousand–plus pounds and are strong enough to plow fields or carry a full-grown man for miles. Yet, the horse is controlled with one small piece of metal called a bit and a leather bridle that fits over the horse's head. You can harness the

> **Words reflect the true condition of a person's heart and maturity.**

wild strength of a horse with something that a horse could trample. Like the bit and bridle, the rudder on a ship is small in comparison to the ship itself, but it is the rudder that steers the ship one direction or another. Even smaller than the rudder is a tiny spark. Although it is tiny, a spark alone has the ability to start a blaze.

Your tongue, the words you say, steer your life in one direction or another. Like the spark, one offhand remark can do major damage. Words reflect the true condition of a person's heart and maturity. Make sure your verbal contributions are uplifting, encouraging, and honest.

Be the one to spread good news about others. Use your words to build people up. Your carefully chosen words can even heal someone who is hurting.

Faith means being sure of the things we hope for and knowing that something is real even if we do not see it.

HEBREWS 11:1 NCV

Attempting to Define Faith

Faith isn't an easy word to define because faith is an indefinable quality that goes beyond words. The New Testament was originally written in the Greek language. In that original text it said that *faith* is "the substance of things hoped and the evidence of things not seen." The word *substance* in Greek is *hupostatis*, which means a structure under something, a foundation, a steadfastness of mind. Faith is the firm foundation on which you rest everything you know about God.

The Bible provides knowledge and history about God. It is filled with truth that is not changed by circumstances. The Bible clearly states who God is, that he is truth and holiness. He doesn't change. Knowing who God is and knowing about his character is not enough. The Bible says even demons know who God is.

Without faith you would be limited to the here and now. You would know God only by what you could see, hear, touch, taste, and smell. There is so much about God that goes beyond your limited human senses. No one was present for creation. It was something God did alone. The Holy Spirit is unseen and can't be touched or heard or smelled or tasted. You can't use your own abilities to define and know faith. Faith is grounded in the truth of the Bible. Faith is accepting your experience with God while combining it with the certainty of the Bible.

> **Faith is accepting your experience with God while combining it with the certainty of the Bible.**

Are you putting your faith in what you can see with your eyes, or in what you know to be true from the Bible? Faith isn't just wishful thinking. It's substantial. It's strong enough to build a life on.

Do not be fooled: "Bad friends will ruin good habits."

1 CORINTHIANS 15:33 NCV

Friends Reflect Who You Are

Friendships are usually based on acceptance. You will gravitate toward the people who accept you. Acceptance could cause your friends to choose you rather than you choosing your friends. Make a conscious effort to choose your friends rather than just choosing acceptance.

Real friends don't just accept you, they love you. Friends have each other's best interests at heart. Friends care enough to be honest and to build each other up. A true friend will risk losing you as a friend in order to confront issues in your life that are harmful or destructive to you. A true friend will value you more than the friendship.

Your friends have more influence on you than anyone else in your life. Just ask Cole. He hangs his head and admit that he can make the right choices, until he gets around a certain group of friends. They make it too easy and daring to do the wrong thing. Friends who share your standards and your

> **Your friends have more influence on you than anyone else in your life.**

beliefs will encourage you in a positive way. Friends who don't share your standards and beliefs are more likely to cause you to fall away from your beliefs than to rise up to yours. You can influence friends who don't know about God by including them in your circle of godly friends rather than spending all your time with their friends. Choose your friends wisely.

Friends are a reflection of who you are and what you stand for. Good friends can bring out the best in you. Take time to evaluate whom you are friends with and why.

We know that a person is made right with God not by following the law, but by trusting in Jesus Christ. So we, too, have put our faith in Christ Jesus, that we might be made right with God because we trusted in Christ. It is not because we followed the law, because no one can be made right with God by following the law.

GALATIANS 2:16 NCV

Follow Jesus

Think about the rules that govern behavior in your school. They help teachers and administrators maintain order by giving them a standard to hold students' conduct against. Most students are there to learn and to get along with their peers, but for those who don't share that attitude, the rules serve as an external motivation to behave as if they did. If all students treated their teachers and fellow students with love, always treated others the way they would want to be treated themselves, there would be no need for rules.

Of course, since nobody's perfect, rules are necessary. But even if the rules can cause people to behave well, no set of rules can make much change on the inside of a person. Not even God's laws do that. God's laws are a stadard for how you should behave toward other people. If you follow the laws of

> **If you obey God's law perfectly, you will behave like a perfectly loving human being.**

God, you will be doing your part toward creating a just and orderly world. If you obey God's laws perfectly, you will behave like a perfectly loving human being.

But the laws of God serve another purpose. They show you how far you have to go. Every time you break one of God's laws—and you will—you are faced with the fact that you can't do it on your own. You see that you need a new heart. Only God can reach into your life and make you into the kind of person the laws say you ought to be.

Trust Jesus to give you a new heart—a heart that truly desires to follow God's laws.

We know that in everything God works for the good of those who love him. They are the people he called, because that was his plan.

ROMANS 8:28 NCV

God's Plans Are Good

Imagine Jake's surprise when, in his junior year of high school, his parents announce that his dad will be interviewing for a new job. Jake is a star player on the football team and actively involved at school. He has a great group of friends who are looking forward to doing their senior year up in a big way. It's tough to see how a move to another city during his senior year could possibly be in Jake's best interest.

Romans 8:28 refers to the kind of good that ultimately glorifies God. If a situation causes you to draw closer to God, it can be identified as good. Paul wrote this in a letter to a group of people in Rome who believed in Jesus but whom he had never met. He wrote the letter to encourage them and to clearly state the truth about Jesus. He wanted to affirm to his readers that God was good and that all of the things that happen in life play a part in God's plan. God's goodness for you includes more than just temporary happiness or granting your immediate wish.

> God's goodness for you includes more than just temporary happiness or granting your immediate wish.

God's good is for the long term. It might include a lesson in patience and endurance during a time when you are being tested. God's good may even include suffering that results in a stronger character or a more compassionate heart. God takes every part of your life and uses it for the ongoing good of your life and his plans.

Like jagged chunks of colored glass, God puts the pieces of your life together to form a radiant and beautiful stainedglass window. God can make your life a work of art.

Every good action and every perfect gift is from God. These good gifts come down from the Creator of the sun, moon, and stars, who does not change like their shifting shadows.

JAMES 1:17 NCV

Good Things

It is important to be clear about what comes from God and what does not. The good that happens in life comes from God. The bad comes either from Satan or from your choice to do something opposite of what is pleasing to God. What comes from God is a result of his flawless judgment and is given from a pure spirit of love.

The Greek word for *perfect* in James 1:17 is defined as "finished, wanting for nothing, brought to an end, complete." God's good may be a process rather than an immediate response or action. That is, this process may involve a complex set of actions and events to bring your good to fruition. If you rely

> God's good may be a process rather than an immediate response or action.

on God while you endure what may seem like a bad process, you are likely to find that when it is over you are more complete and wanting for nothing.

The kind of good that God gives is distinct from the good anyone else would give. The kind of good that comes from God encompasses not just right now, but all space and time. His good is based on more than the circumstance you might find yourself in. In the midst of a painful situation, you may question why all this bad stuff had to happen to you. What you may or may not realize is that God did not cause any of the bad stuff to happen, but that he can use the bad stuff for good if you allow him to.

~

Don't let the bad stuff in life make you doubt the goodness of God. His plan is to give you the best things in life.

I don't care about my own life. The most important thing is that I complete my mission, the work that the Lord Jesus gave me—to tell people the Good News about God's grace.

ACTS 20:24 NCV

Worth Telling About

Paul prepared to go to a place where he knew he would be imprisoned and beaten, maybe even killed, for his beliefs. None of these things deterred him from going. Paul would rather face pain and imprisonment than give up his task of telling people about Jesus. To Paul life was worthless if he couldn't be telling others about Jesus.

Paul knew that without Jesus in their lives, people would be separated from God forever. And being separated from God prevented them from living life to the fullest. It was the most important thing people needed to know.

In some countries today there are places where it is illegal to talk about your faith in Jesus. The Christian Church functions in underground home churches. There are even places where pastors and Christians are imprisoned for talking about their faith. At the same time, the number of new Christians is growing at an astounding rate in these places. The

> **The assurance that a person's life counts for something—that there is a God who loves them—is the greatest gift.**

people in those countries know that it is worth risking their lives to spread the love of God. They know that God introduces forgiveness and mercy into life as they embrace the unconditional love he offers. In good times and in bad, the assurance that a person's life counts for something—that there is a God who loves them—is the greatest gift.

Someone is dying to know about the love of God. Share what you know about God.

The Lord is not slow in doing what he promised—the way some people understand slowness. But God is being patient with you. He does not want anyone to be lost, but he wants all people to change their hearts and lives.

2 PETER 3:9 NCV

Waiting for Everyone

Peter addressed the complacency developing in the early church. He explained that God's timetable was a benefit, not a problem. Your concept of time is different from God's. In your life everything has a beginning and an end. God is timeless, able to be in all time—past, present, and future. When Jesus left the earth to return to his Father God, he promised he would return soon to establish the kingdom of heaven on earth. Many of his followers believed his return would be in their lifetime.

When the first generation of believers passed away, the next generation started questioning when Jesus would return. This opened the door

> **It's the time to be intentional about telling everyone you know about God.**

for all kinds of doubt. With the door open, false information crept in that didn't stick to the Scripture and teaching established by the first-generation believers. Peter wanted the church to be patient and wait for God's timing.

Peter's reasoning included the fact that the longer they waited for God to return, the more time there was to spread God's message. More people could join the family of God. This isn't the time to sit around and wait for God to return. It's the time to be intentional about telling everyone you know about God. At some moment in time God is going to return. When he does, it will be too late for any person who hasn't come to know God. Prepare to go to heaven and take as many people as you can with you.

~🙙🙛~

Is there someone you love or care for who has still not accepted the invitation to become a part of God's family? Extend the invitation to them today.

Always be willing to listen and slow to speak. Do not become angry easily.

JAMES 1:19 NCV

Listen Up

Think how much time you spend trying to explain yourself—trying to make your parents see your side of the curfew issue, telling your friends how you feel, making your case during a class discussion. Everybody wants to be understood. You want to express your opinion, and even if people don't agree with your view of things, you at least want them to know where you're coming from.

The Bible teaches that your first move should be to listen, not to talk. When you're talking, it feels like you're getting the upper hand in a discussion. But you gain knowledge by opening your ears, not by opening your mouth. And knowledge is power, isn't it? A willingness to listen doesn't reflect weakness. It reflects the strength of wisdom. Listening demonstrates a willingness to arrive at a conclusion that makes sense for everybody involved. And if it's necessary to "win" an argument, by the way, listening before talking is excellent strategy. But if you're wise, winning is rarely your first concern in a conversation.

If you listen—if you seek to understand—you will be slow to anger. Talking has a tendency to convince you of your own rightness (even

> A willingness to listen doesn't reflect weakness. It reflects the strength of wisdom.

if it doesn't convince the person you're talking to), and self-righteousness makes you impatient with other people's opinions and quick to anger. So listen. Understand. Then you'll be ready to make yourself understood.

Next time you find yourself running off at the mouth, stop, look, and listen.

> Whoever opposes the existing authority opposes what God has ordered; and anyone who does so will bring judgment on himself.

ROMANS 13:2 GNT

Freedom Under God

Real freedom in life is found when you understand your relationship to the people in authority. God places authority in your life; rebelling against authority is rebelling against God. It's important to clearly understand how your response to authority affects your relationship with God.

Think of the authorities God has placed in your life: parents, teachers, government authorities, police, laws, covenants, and more. God placed authority in your life to guide you, direct you, challenge you, keep you safe, make you think, and help you. If a police officer pulls you over for doing 55 mph in a 35 mph school zone and gives you a ticket that costs you $100, you may feel like the officer, the law, and the ticket are imposing restrictions on your freedom. After all, you know how to drive safely, and 55 mph is not that fast. But it is too fast in that par-

> **God places authority in your life; rebelling against authority is rebelling against God.**

ticular situation. What would happen if in that same school zone you did not see a little girl dart across the crosswalk? At 55 mph, you might not be able to stop in time.

The bottom line is that when you choose to evaluate which rules or requests you are going to follow and which you are not, you make yourself the authority. You end up damaging your relationship with God and the people he placed in authority in your life. Freedom from authority has a cost—it's called consequences. When you resist God's authority, you resist the One who loves you the most.

Do you respect the authorities that God has placed in your life? If not, you're rebelling against more than human author-ity; you're rebelling against God's authority, too.

Whoever loves money will never have enough money; whoever loves wealth will not be satisfied with it.

ECCLESIASTES 5:10 NCV

Satisfaction

Remember how cool your mobile phone was when you first got it? How long did it take before you decided that it wasn't cool enough and wanted to replace it with a newer model? It doesn't take long for mobile phones or computers or clothes or cars to seem so five-minutes-ago. It's on to the newer model, or you're going to be left behind. That's the way it goes with material things. They're never good enough. Not for long, anyway. If you get the thing you think you want, you find that what you've really done is simply graduated to a desire for something a little newer, nicer, and more expensive.

God is the fulfillment of all your desires. And he gives himself freely to you. The more you have of God, the more you want of him: in that regard, the desire for God is like other desires. The difference is that as your desire for God grows, he gladly gives you more of himself. When was the last time a new laptop gave itself freely to you? Objects are simply that—objects. Nothing more.

> Contentment is a decision to be happy with what God has provided.

When people chase after money, they are really searching for contentment. Contentment doesn't come from having more stuff, however. It comes from enjoying what you have already. Contentment is a decision to be happy with what God has provided. It comes from being thankful for the good things in your life. The more you appreciate what you already have, the less time you will spend trying to get more.

Try starting a list of things you are thankful for. Each day write down two or three things you are grateful for. Include at least one thing money can't buy.

The fruit of the Spirit is love, joy, peace, longsuffering, kindness, goodness, faithfulness, gentleness, self-control.

GALATIANS 5:22–23 NKJV

Good Fruit

You might know Christians who are uptight and judgmental, or Christians who give the impression that following Jesus must not be very much fun. Maybe you're one of them. When the Holy Spirit enters a person's life, that person begins to bear a new kind of fruit. And it isn't the fruit of self-righteousness or a gloomy determination to "stick to the rules." No, the fruit of the Spirit is love, joy, peace, patience, kindness, goodness, faithfulness, gentleness, and self-control.

To walk in the Spirit is to be set apart, distinct. You are distinguished by a loving spirit; you can afford to love others because you're beginning to know how much God loves you.

You are distinguished by a greater joy and fulfillment than the people around you. When you are set apart, you begin to take the world less seriously than everyone around you because, in

> **You can afford to love others because you're beginning to know how much God loves you.**

the end, you take something else much more seriously than the world. And that means you can be patient with the shortcomings of the people around you. Because you know that God is looking out for you, you can be kind and good and gentle rather than looking out for number one. Because you know there's much more to life than self-gratification, you can be self-controlled rather than self-indulgent.

But don't expect to do any of that in your own strength. This is the fruit of the Spirit, not the fruit of human beings. Only the Spirit can cause you to bear that kind of fruit.

What kind of fruit are you bearing? If the fruit of the Spirit doesn't characterize your life, you'd better reevaluate your walk.

Even if you have to suffer for doing good things, God will bless you. So stop being afraid and don't worry about what people might do.

1 Peter 3:14 cev

Do the Good Thing

You've heard of Christians in other countries who go through great danger for the sake of the gospel. Worship services are interrupted by gun-wielding militants. Christians are threatened with death if they don't renounce their faith. Christians are denied jobs and other opportunities simply because they're Christians. How about you? Have you ever suffered because someone was making fun of the gospel? Probably nobody's ever threatened you and demanded that you renounce your faith. But you have, no doubt, been in situations where you're tempted to deny Christ by going along, by pretending your faith was unimportant to you for the sake of fitting in. Maybe you've missed a starting position because you wouldn't skip church for a Sunday practice or game. This sort of unfairness is sometimes subtle, and many times people don't even realize when they've put you in a sticky situation, but the principle is

> **In this country, persecution is much more subtle than a machine gun.**

the same: you have to decide whether or not to deny Christ and go the way of the world.

The Bible promises that if you suffer for doing good, God will bless you. If you're trading in your consistent walk for the sake of popularity or a starting spot on the varsity, you're missing out on God's blessing. You've got nothing to fear from other people. Do you really fear other people's disapproval more than you fear God's? Would you really prefer to live a life of cowardice rather than a life of blessing?

There are many worse things than being persecuted— whether intentionally or unintentionally—for your faith. Don't fear what people can do to you. You have God on your side.

Let us run the race that is before us and never give up. We should remove from our lives anything that would get in the way and the sin that so easily holds us back.

HEBREWS 12:1 NCV

Don't Stop

In addition to the athletes on a track team, there is a coach. The coach evaluates the condition of each athlete's form and physical condition. He is responsible for helping the athlete improve his race performance, which includes disciplining and correcting the athlete. The author of Hebrews suggests that you look at your relationship with God from the perspective of a runner in a race with God as your coach.

Like the runner in a race, set your sights on the finish line, which in your case is the end of your life on earth. Set a training schedule that includes spiritual discipline. Prayer and worship are two spiritual disciplines you may be familiar with. Fasting is also a spiritual discipline you may have heard of; fasting is the decision to give up something that is important to you for a set period of time in order to focus on God. For instance, you could give up your favorite TV program for a month and use the time to do a Bible study.

> **Stick to a good training schedule, and, above all, listen to your coach—God.**

If your goal is to stay on track with your relationship to God, then be like the runner and do not let anything distract you from getting to the finish line. Take the time to figure out what might get you off track in your relationship with God. Get rid of the things that tear down your relationship with him, and allow only those things that build it up. Stick to a good training schedule, and, above all, listen to your coach—God.

If you aren't in training, you can't hope to be much of a racer. Get serious about seeking God: keep your eyes on Jesus, and the finish line.

God's word is alive and working and is sharper than a double-edged sword. It cuts all the way into us, where the soul and the spirit are joined, to the center of our joints and bones. And it judges the thoughts and feelings in our hearts.

HEBREWS 4:12 NCV

The Challenge of Scripture

You are blessed to live in a time when worship leaders, youth pastors, musicians, and authors are working hard to make the Bible relevant to people your age. Contemporary worship services, youth sermons, Christian music, and books like this one all try to put the truths of the gospel in terms that make sense to people like you. But it's important to remember that in the end, human beings don't make God relevant. God makes human beings relevant. Your leaders may conform the message to your lifestyle and interests, but ultimately the point is that your lifestyle and interests need to conform to the message. It's a matter of proper alignment of you in relation to God.

The Bible isn't a dead document. It's alive, and it makes you alive. It cuts through all the protective layers that you hide beneath and hits you exactly where you live. It deals with you at the very center of your being and says, in effect, "Here. This is how you are to

> **The Bible isn't a dead document. It's alive, and it makes you alive.**

live. This is what pleases God. This is what will make you happy and fulfilled."

Life is tricky and very complicated. The good life is not the sort of thing you can figure out on your own. But living Scripture gives you a standard to pattern your life after. Do you want to be totally alive, totally relevant? Look in the Bible.

Are you living your life on the surface, or all the way down to the bones and marrow? The Bible challenges you in your deepest self.

They traded the truth of God for a lie. They worshiped and served what had been created instead of the God who created those things, who should be praised forever.

Worship God

Worship is your reverence, your honor toward something. Worship is committing your life to whatever you love the most. Worship is more than a church service or music. Worship is a lifestyle that reflects with honor the One you love the most.

Paul, the writer of Romans, retold the tragedy of what happened in the Old Testament when Christians became frustrated or impatient with God. If God didn't do what they thought he should, they found other things to worship. As a result, they drifted away from God. They became consumed by their own selfish desires. Paul warned the Christians in Rome to worship God and not the things God created for them.

> You can choose to make the most ordinary tasks in your day an act of worship by doing them with excellence.

The Bible tells about all kinds of ways people worshiped God. Worship in Bible times included Scripture reading, music, teaching, dancing, extended periods of silence, and prayer. Praise music and friends all around can enhance a worship experience, but worship is more than the experience. Worship is your response to God's power and grace and love. If you truly love God, your worship of him will overflow into your daily life. Your words and your actions will become a form of worship to God. You can choose to make the most ordinary tasks in your day an act of worship by doing them with excellence.

Worship God when you brush your teeth in the morning; teeth are a gift from God. Worship God when you lay your head on your pillow tonight; thank him for another day.

Run away from sexual sin. Every other sin people do is outside their bodies, but those who sin sexually sin against their own bodies. You should know that your body is a temple for the Holy Spirit who is in you. You have received the Holy Spirit from God. So you do not belong to yourselves.

1 CORINTHIANS 6:18–19 NCV

Worth the Wait

You're tired of waiting for a cake to come out of the oven, so you decide to snatch it out and dip into the half-baked batter with a spoon. If someone prevented you from carrying out your plan, you might consider that person a party pooper, intent on spoiling your fun. But isn't it just as likely that this person, instead of trying to spoil your enjoyment of the cake, is actually trying to enhance it? You might think you want cake batter, but that's just because you aren't in touch with how good cake can be when it's done right. If you wait for the cake to be ready, you'll be very glad you did.

You live in a highly sexualized culture. From the things you see on television and movies to the articles in magazines to the clothes your peers wear, sex— however you can get it—is portrayed as the key to personal fulfillment and self-expression. So when you learn that the Bible forbids sex outside marriage, you might perceive God as a cosmic party pooper determined to spoil the fun of sex.

> The Bible doesn't teach that sex is bad. It teaches that it's good— too good to be thrown away.

But isn't it possible that God is just the opposite? Maybe God's laws are designed to heighten your enjoyment of sex by ensuring that you don't settle for a cheapened, half-baked version. The Bible doesn't teach that sex is bad. It teaches that it's good—too good to be thrown away. Sex is good enough to be worth the wait.

One of the greatest gifts God gives is sexual intimacy within a marriage. It is your job to protect that gift for your future marriage partner.

Jesus said to me, "My grace is enough for you. When you are weak, my power is made perfect in you." So I am very happy to brag about my weaknesses. Then Christ's power can live in me.

2 Corinthians 12:9 NCV

He Can Use Your Weakness

Paul discovered the secret to dealing with the unpleasant things in life. He decided to treat his weakness and difficulties as a gift from God. He could do this because he realized the weaker he became, the more he had to depend on God's strength. Paul asked God to take away his weakness, but God chose to leave it. Paul's weakness strengthened his relationship with God. God did not take Paul's difficulties away; God helped Paul deal with them.

Difficulties and challenges are a good thing; they are opportunities to allow God to do things he wouldn't otherwise do. You may face difficulties in your life that you wish God would just take away. God may supply what you need to make it through your difficulties rather than remove them. For example, a father will take his child to the doctor and allow that child to be given what appears to the child as a big,

> **God may supply what you need to make it through your difficulties rather than remove them.**

painful shot. A child will not understand why his father allowed someone to hurt him until he is older and realizes that shots can make you well or keep you from getting sick. Remember that God sees beyond your moment of suffering.

When you ask for God's help, you gain the chance to see all the things he can do. Take your difficulties and weaknesses to God in prayer. Ask him to use them in a way that reveals his strength and greatness.

You may think of your point of weakness as the last place where God can work through your life. Have you ever considered the possibility that it might be the precise spot where God plans to work? Commit even your weaknesses and failures to God's good work.

All Scripture is given by inspiration of God, and is profitable for doctrine, for reproof, for correction, for instruction in righteousness.

2 TIMOTHY 3:16 NKJV

God's Word Can Do It

The words in the Bible may have been written by the hands of men like Moses, Paul, Peter, and Jeremiah, but the words came from God. God is the author of the Bible. In the Bible, you will read about individual people, history, nations, kings, disaster, and triumph. God used all these things to reveal his plan for the world and for your life. The words in the Bible are from God to you. As Paul told Timothy, the Scriptures equip you for every kind of situation where God places you.

You can count on the Scripture to be your guide as you make decisions. The words will direct you to make positive changes in your life. The Bible will become your manual for worship, for relationships, and for life. As a follower of God you will be empowered by the Holy Spirit to read, study, and learn the Bible in a way you never thought possible. The Bible is

> **You can count on the Scripture to be your guide as you make decisions.**

the ultimate guide and inspiration for anything you want to accomplish and everything you need to understand. Search the Bible, and you will find great advice and tips for every aspect of your life.

Because the words in the Bible come from God, you can trust what you read and learn from it. Paul warned Timothy of a time to come in the future when the validity of the Scripture would come into question. Paul wanted Timothy to know that the Scripture was not only valid and true, but that it also would be of value in every age to come. It is the first and last word of truth from God in all circumstances.

What are you basing your decisions on? If you're basing them on anything other than the Word of God, you're asking for trouble.

Do not change yourselves to be like the people of this world, but be changed within by a new way of thinking. Then you will be able to decide what God wants for you; you will know what is good and pleasing to him and what is perfect.

ROMANS 12:2 NCV

Go Against the Grain

Once you identify yourself as someone who follows God, your life should undergo a change. Your mind will start to think about things from God's perspective. Paul suggested to the Christians in Rome that they look to God and not to their culture for guidance about how they should live. In his letter, Paul encouraged the Christians in Rome to live differently because of their beliefs.

Which TV shows should you watch? Should you or shouldn't you see a PG-13 or an R-rated movie? What kind of music should you listen to? How should you treat people? How far is too far on a date? A lot of things are popularly accepted that may or may not be in line with what the Bible says is acceptable; reading your Bible and praying will help you decide, based on God's principles, what you should do.

> **A lot of things are popularly accepted that may or may not be in line with what the Bible says is acceptable.**

You will face decisions that are not always black or white. Paul's words are there for you today. Like the Christians in Rome, hold yourself to God's standards. Your choices might not match the popular majority; you might have to miss out on certain movies or skip certain concerts because you know what you see or hear would not be pleasing to God. It's okay to say, "That's not a good choice for me." You will feel peace when you do things according to God's standard.

Go against the grain by questioning what is commonly acceptable and by making choices that reflect biblical principles. Live out your beliefs. Stand firmly for what God shows you to be the right thing for you.

It is worth nothing for them to have the whole world if they lose their souls.

MARK 8:36 NCV

All for Nothing

Jesus predicted the hardships his followers would face as a result of his death. He tried to impress on his followers the irreplaceable value of knowing, for sure, for themselves, that Jesus is the Son of God. Jesus was keenly aware of all the things that would tempt his followers to deny their belief in him. They would confront ridicule and the fear of being tortured for their beliefs. They would grow tired of serving others. They would rationalize holding on to the things they wanted. They would risk destroying their relationship with God.

The term is *selling out*. When the stakes get too high or the pressure gets too great or the money gets big, the temptation to sell out is there. Selling out is deliberately putting aside your core values and beliefs in exchange for something that seems more desirable.

There are at least two common situations that will bait you into selling out. The first one occurs when you feel the pressure to fit in, blend in, and not stand out. No one likes being pegged as weird or different. The second involves money or fame. The desire for a chance at big

> **Jesus was keenly aware of all the things that would tempt his followers to deny their belief in him.**

money or a large amount of personal attention could cause you to set aside or reorder your priorities. In both situations you could be tempted to downplay your beliefs or even compromise them. Remember, there isn't one single thing in this world that would ever be worth sacrificing God's lifelong love for you.

Don't be a sellout. Don't trade the riches of God's kingdom for the cheap pleasures of earth.

> **I**f two of you on earth agree about something and pray for it, it will be done for you by my Father in heaven.

MATTHEW 18:19 NCV

Pray with a Friend

Jesus knew the end of his time on earth was near. With time running out there were a few important things he wanted the disciples to know and to understand without a doubt. The disciples had witnessed many miracles. They were there when a blind man was healed and made to see again. They were the ones who brought Jesus the five loaves of bread and five fish that fed more than five thousand people. It was important for the disciples to understand that the power of healing and the miracle of the loaves and fishes came from God, who is always present. God's power would not disappear when Jesus returned to heaven.

It is important for you, too, to understand this concept. What you and your friends agree on in prayer will carry the authority of God. God's authority can defeat poverty, drugs, and gangs. It can bring healing and change in the lives of the people at

> **There is strength in numbers, especially when a number of Christians pray.**

your school, in your city, and in your community. There is strength in numbers, especially when a number of Christians pray.

Sharing your prayers with another person is different from praying to God by yourself. By praying with a friend or a group of friends, you gain one another's strength and resolve. Praying with friends reinforces your belief that God will answer you when you pray. Praying together also unifies you and your friends. As a unified group of believers, you and your friends will be more effective at sharing God's love.

When you come together with friends to pray, it is like a holy army protecting your school, your neighborhood, and your family. Contact some friends today and plan to pray together.

If two of you on earth
agree about something
and pray for it, it will be
done for you by my
Father in heaven.

MATTHEW 18:19 NCV

W hoever can be trusted with a little can also be trusted with a lot, and whoever is dishonest with a little is dishonest with a lot.

LUKE 16:10 NCV

Honesty Counts

It's pouring down rain, and you are late to school. The cashier at the fast-food drive-up window gives you an extra dollar in change. Parking your car and running the dollar back to the cashier is an example of being honest in the little things. After school, another friend has a new CD you want, but can't afford. Your friend offers to burn you a copy, but you decline, even though you know you probably would never get caught or arrested for it.

You could rationalize burning a copy of your friend's new CD by committing to buy a copy when you have the money. The bottom line is that burning CDs is against the law no matter how you rationalize it.

Daily life presents situations where you will have to decide, not only whether or not to be honest, but how honest. Do you take the gold bracelet you found to the lost-and-found? Of course! Do you pocket the cash you found in the any-time teller? No way!

> **Daily life presents situations where you will have to decide, not only whether or not to be honest, but how honest.**

The standard of honesty you set for your life will be noticed by others. At the same time, God will trust you with greater responsibilities and opportunities for sharing with others. Not burning that CD you really wanted may be the first step in getting a friend interested in what it means to be a Christian.

If you want people to listen to what you have to say about God, you have to prove yourself believable and trustworthy in all areas of your life.

All people will know that you are my followers if you love each other.

JOHN 13:35 NCV

Be Known by Your Love

In the Old Testament, the people of God followed laws designed to help them be holy and to set them apart from other religions. There were laws for every aspect of life to ensure that people were doing their best to live a holy and separate life. These requirements failed to keep God's people separate. They lost their meaning and became routine. Jesus gave a new law or command that summed up the Old Testament law: love others. Your friends and family will know you are a follower of God by how you love people.

Scientific research suggests that every human being requires love, but you don't need scientists to tell you that. The evidence is up and down the hallways of your school. People display their need for love in a variety of ways, from clothes that stand out to the R-rated displays

> **Loving others will set you apart far more than any Christian symbol, jewelry, or T-shirt you can wear.**

of public affection. Anyone with an authentic love for other people will get noticed.

Loving others will set you apart far more than any Christian symbol, jewelry, or T-shirt you can wear. Love isn't something you talk about; it's something you do when you treat everyone equally. Real love happens when you take time to listen to someone who is hurting. Being a good listener and offering to pray with someone about a problem shows love too. Love others in the same unrestricted way God loves you, and leave no doubt about your relationship with God.

When you love people without any conditions or exceptions, people will notice. Let love for others be your ID.

We have this treasure from God, but we are like clay jars that hold the treasure. This shows that the great power is from God, not from us.

2 CORINTHIANS 4:7 NCV

Earthen Vessels

You might have seen one of those action-adventure movies where everybody spends the whole movie looking for a hidden map or a hidden jewel or a hidden key, only to discover in the end that it is in a clay flowerpot or a beat-up old chest the whole time. The treasure is hidden in the most unlikely of places—not in a satin-lined padded case with titanium locks and armed guards, but in plain sight, where nobody would think to look.

God is clever like that. He hides the treasure of his gospel in the most unlikely places: in normal people like you. When God became a human being, he became a lowly carpenter's son, not a great earthly king. When he gathered up disciples, he recruited fishermen and laborers, not the rich and powerful. And he's still

> **There's nothing average about average people.**

doing the same. Sure, there are rich and powerful people in the kingdom of God. But they are outnumbered by the regular people—jars of clay in which the greatest of all treasures is hidden.

You may feel like nobody special—painfully average. You may be hoping just to get up to the level of average. That doesn't disqualify you from serving God. Average people are God's specialty. Or to put it another way, there's nothing average about average people. God isn't looking for people who have it all figured out. If such people actually existed, why would they need God? No, God is looking for people like you.

Let go of self-pity. God hides his greatest treasure in clay pots like you, not in fancy treasure chests.

Then Jesus told him, "You believe because you see me. Those who believe without seeing me will be truly happy."

Not Seeing Is Believing

Christians believe in the existence of something that can't be seen. You already believe in the existence of at least one thing you can't see. You believe there is air without seeing it. If you didn't believe it was available you would live in panic, wondering where your next breath was coming from.

A blind man in the Bible could not see Jesus, but he went to him to be healed. He heard that Jesus was healing people, and the blind man wanted to see. After Jesus died and came back to life, his disciples wanted to see him to confirm that he was really alive. One of his disciples, Thomas, would not believe anyone who told him Jesus was alive. Thomas did not believe Jesus had risen from the dead until he placed his hand into Jesus's side where a spear had pierced him. The blind man believed in Jesus even though he couldn't see him.

The blind man listened to the stories about Jesus. He gathered all the information he could and then went to where Jesus was. He asked Jesus to heal him. The blind man accepted that Jesus was who he said he was, the Savior and the Son of God, and that he had the power to heal. Faith is accepting the truth

> Thomas did not believe Jesus had risen from the dead until he placed his hand into Jesus's side where a spear had pierced him.

found in the Bible. The Bible will provide the truth you need about Jesus and about God. If you believe it, accept it, and live your life as though you believe it, that is faith.

Seeing may be believing, but are you ready to believe in something that you haven't seen? When it comes to the Christian faith, believing is seeing.

After the earthquake a fire, but the LORD was not in the fire; and after the fire a still small voice.

1 KINGS 19:12 NKJV

Where Is God?

When you're surfing the Web, have you ever noticed that the blinkiest, brightest, most obnoxiously animated banner ads are the ones that direct you to the most worthless Web sites? Have you ever noticed that the guy who yells the loudest on the television ads is the guy who's trying to sell you something you don't need? When God spoke to Elijah, he didn't speak in the earthquake or the fire. He spoke to him in a small voice—not the kind of voice that forces you to hear, but the kind of voice you have to be listening for.

If God doesn't speak loudly, it would be good to set aside a quiet time to hear him. God's voice is the understanding and knowledge that come from reading the Bible and from praying. It's a sense of assurance that comes from spending time with God. You know God is speaking when you get a kind of peace that is out of the

> You know God is speaking when you get a kind of peace that is out of the ordinary and beyond the realities of whatever is happening around you.

ordinary and beyond the realities of whatever is happening around you.

Someday God may choose to speak to you in a voice as loud as an earthquake. You may see him as brightly as a burning fire. Perhaps he already has spoken to you that clearly. That's not how he usually speaks, however. The life of consistent faith requires that you sit still long enough to hear God whisper.

Find a quiet time and place to read your Bible and pray. Ask God to teach you to hear his voice; as you take the time to listen you will learn to hear God's voice.

God can do anything! . . . You are blessed because you believed that what the Lord said to you would really happen.

LUKE 1:37, 45 NCV

Dream Big

"Nothing is impossible for God" were the words spoken to a young girl named Mary by an angel sent from God. What the angel told Mary seemed impossible and beyond her wildest dreams, but it happened. Mary—a teenager, engaged but not married, a virgin bride-to-be—became the mother of the Son of God. Her mind told her it was impossible, but the baby moving inside her was a constant reminder that with God nothing is impossible. God made the impossible possible.

The surprising way God chose to bring his Son, Jesus, into the world stands as a reminder to you that nothing is beyond God's abilities. Nothing is beyond God's imagination and vision. God can pull substance from nothing. God can transform something dull and nondescript to something spectacular. God uses ordinary people to do the unbelievable. God made it possible for three believers to survive walking around in a fiery furnace. God made it possible for Daniel to be lowered into a pit of hungry lions but not be eaten alive. God made it possible for Noah to build a boat and coax a pair of every animal on earth to go inside. God made it possible for Jesus to raise his friend Lazarus from the dead. God's skills are limitless.

> **God uses ordinary people to do the unbelievable.**

The list of possibilities for who you can be, what you can accomplish, or where you can go has no limits and will never end. That's what is so great about knowing God and being in a relationship with him—it makes your world a lot bigger.

Be ready to take part in God's grand design. "Impossible" means nothing to God. Do you have the faith to see God's reality?

I heard the voice of the Lord, saying:
"Whom shall I send, and who will go for
Us?" Then I said, "Here am I! Send me."

ISAIAH 6:8 NKJV

Send Me

When you have some good news—a big sale at the mall, a new band you've discovered, a big win for your favorite team—you don't hesitate to tell people. Are you just as eager to tell people the news that God loves them and has a plan for their lives? When God asked the prophet Isaiah to go and tell people about the God who loved them, Isaiah realized his job wouldn't be easy. It would require sacrifice and make him unpopular at times. Nevertheless, Isaiah said yes to God.

God asks you to go and tell other people about him. You may not have to go far, possibly just into your own living room to tell someone in your family about God. You may get the opportunity to tell a friend at school about God. Telling others about God doesn't involve only words. Sure, talking about God is a great way to let others know about him. But you can also let others know about God by your actions. You can share God's message by lending a hand in your own city. You might go to a food

> **If you respond to God and say, "Send me," God will go with you.**

bank and help unload donated food for the poor people in your city. You may even be challenged to go on a mission trip to another country.

If you respond to God and say, "Send me," God will go with you. God will be there when you talk to your family and friends and when you work in your community. God will be along for the ride if you decide to go on a mission trip. Your willingness to put God's plans for your life before your own is the response God will be looking for.

Start planning a way to put your belief in God into action. Include in your action plan a list of people in your life right now who might not know about God's love.

My body and my mind may become weak, but God is my strength. He is mine forever.

When All Else Fails

D.J. is 17 and has Type I diabetes. For the rest of his life he must have medication to stay alive. There's nothing fun about poking your finger several times a day with a needle to check your blood sugar levels. D.J.'s fingers are pretty important to him since he plays guitar. Worship or rock, the music D.J. plays and the lyrics he sings reflect his passion for God.

The writer of Psalm 73 also had a passion for God. It seemed no matter how hard he tried to do things right, everything just kept going wrong. It was as if other people, who didn't know God, ended up better off than he was. D.J. struggled with the same issue when he first got sick. Why was his body weak? After all, he was a good kid who loved God. But eventually D.J. realized what the psalmist realized: even in weakness, God is his rock. Even though the people who don't honor God may appear to be healthier or wealthier, there will come a day when knowing God is more valuable.

> **Even though the people who don't honor God may appear to be healthier or wealthier, there will come a day when knowing God is more valuable.**

In Psalm 73:6 the Hebrew word for *strength* is a form of the word *rock*. *Strength* is defined as the "rock of God." Bad stuff happens in life, and not just when you've done something wrong. This side of heaven, you may never know why God has put certain challenges in your life. But when you are weak, God is strong.

When things go wrong in your life, God still loves you. His love is a fact, not a feeling, which will never fall apart. His love is rock-solid.

> Trust the LORD with all your heart, and don't depend on your own understanding.

PROVERBS 3:5 NCV

God Knows More Than You Do

Dylan was furious. It was his sixteenth birthday, and he wanted to spend it with his friends. But his parents insisted that he spend the evening with them. Dylan pouted through dinner. The truth is, he was a jerk. He didn't say a word to his parents on the way home from the restaurant. He planned to go straight into his room and close the door behind him.

What a shock when Dylan opened the front door and heard the happy shouts of his friends: "Surprise!!" All at once he realized just how mean he had been. The only reason his parents had insisted on taking him out was so his friends could get things ready for a surprise birthday party. His parents wanted his friends to be there to see him get the keys to his first car. Dylan was almost too ashamed of himself to enjoy it.

Like Dylan, you can't see the whole picture. If you lean on your own understanding, you're going to come to some wrong conclusions. But God does see the big picture. He's got the whole world in his hands. He knows what's best for you. More than that, he desires what's best for you and is able to make it happen, even if that means directing you through things that aren't much fun at the time. The experiences that leave you wanting to grumble and pout are leading you toward the happy surprise of God's good purposes for your life.

> The experiences that leave you wanting to grumble and pout are leading you toward the happy surprise of God's good purposes for your life.

What are you grumbling about? What aspect of your life does God seem to have forgotten about? Give it to God, and trust him.

I call to you, God, and you answer me.
Listen to me now, and hear what I say.

PSALM 17:6 NCV

God Will Answer

If you have ever IM'd a friend, you know what it is to wait and wait and wait . . . The person on the other end can't hear you, and there is no real way to yell or get the person's attention. Sure, you can capitalize every single letter in bold print and add a bunch of exclamation marks, but he still won't actually hear you. But there's no waiting with God. God hears you, and he answers you.

God is interested in hearing about your day, whom you like, what is bugging you, and whatever is on your heart. You never get a BRB or an AFK from God. He never steps way from the computer screen of your heart. He is always online for you.

FYI: Prayer can be your instant message to God. You don't have to worry about getting kicked off-line with God. Prayer is the connection to God that always operates on full power. You have a connection that will result in a response from God. Unlike the friend who steps away from the computer when you ask a critical question or need some real advice, God stays with you all the time. He answers every message you send him, instant or otherwise. Sometimes he will answer you with a verse in the Bible as you read Scripture. Sometimes he will send someone your way to help you see God's answer. Sometimes you will get a sense of peace and a sense of knowing what needs to be done to keep that peace. The fact is, God hears you, and he answers you.

> **You never get a BRB or an AFK from God.**

God is ready to listen to you. Send up a prayer right now; tell him what is on your heart. He will respond to you.

Our light affliction, which is but for a moment, is working for us a far more exceeding and eternal weight of glory.

2 CORINTHIANS 4:17 NKJV

Light Affliction and the Weight of Glory

Life isn't easy. Everybody faces heartache, disappointment, difficulty, pain. Think about your five closest friends. At least one of them is probably going through a breakup, parents splitting up, an addiction, or a failure. Maybe you're going through one or more of those things yourself. When you're suffering, God may seem far away. You may be tempted to quit: if God's not going to protect you from pain any better than that, what's the point?

But God never promised to shield you from hurt. He has, however, promised to give you strength to get through hard times. And more than that, he has promised a glorious future in heaven, so weighty and solid that the sufferings of this life will seem small by comparison. That can seem hard to believe when you're going through a hard time. Nothing seems more real than pain when you're in the middle of it. But God calls you to live by faith, to hold on to the hope of better times, not just in this life, but throughout eternity.

> **Nothing seems more real than pain when you're in the middle of it.**

The cyclist Lance Armstrong said, "Pain is temporary. Quitting lasts forever." When you're in pain, you want to quit. But take care not to let a temporary situation lead you to quit and miss out on the forever of God's joy. In the big scheme of things, your earthly sufferings last only for a moment. So press on.

—◦—

When you're hurting, take the long view. Pain is temporary, but heaven is forever.

We also have as our ambition, whether at home or absent, to be pleasing to Him.

2 Corinthians 5:9 NASB

What Do You Want to Be?

"What do you want to be when you grow up?" People have been asking you that question since you were barely old enough to talk. Chances are, you answer that question differently now than you did when you were little. There's a good chance you'll have yet another answer by the time you finish college and embark on a career. "What do you want to be when you grow up?" is another way of asking, "What are your ambitions?" Ambitions change, and at any one time you have many different ambitions, some of them contradictory. You might want to go to a certain college, get a certain job, marry a certain kind of person, live in a certain kind of place.

Paul said he had only one ambition: to be pleasing to God. Whatever other ambitions Paul might have had, they all answered to that one overruling ambition. How about you? Sure, pleasing God is probably on your list of ambitions. But is it at the top? Do all of your other ambitions answer to that

> **Sure, pleasing God is probably on your list of ambitions. But is it at the top?**

one ambition, or are your spiritual ambitions shaped by other priorities? Put it this way: you have an ambition to succeed, and you have an ambition to please God. If success is your number one priority, you might try to please God because you hope he will bless you with success, however you define it. If pleasing God is your top priority, then that's going to shape your definition of success.

~\|\|\)

What are your ambitions? Will any of those ambitions change if pleasing God becomes your number one ambition?

I give you a new command: Love each other. You must love each other as I have loved you.

JOHN 13:34 NCV

You also be ready, for the Son of Man is coming at an hour you do not expect.

LUKE 12:40 NKJV

Be Ready

No one knows exactly when Jesus will come back to the earth. The Bible does say he will come back, but it does not give a specific date and time. With no specific date and time, you need to be ready all the time.

When Jesus wanted to make sure people remembered what he had to say, he would make his point by illustrating it in a story. To prepare his followers for his return after his death and resurrection, he told a story about a servant who waited for his master to return. When the master returned, the servant was there waiting to immediately open the door for him. Although the servant didn't know the date or time of his master's return, he was prepared at every moment to welcome his master back, whether late into the night or early in the morning.

You can prepare right now for the moment when Jesus comes back. Make your life a place where you would feel proud to welcome Jesus. Choose music that you would be comfortable listening to with Jesus. Talk to your friends and family in a way that would please Jesus if he overheard the conversation. Consider how you might be affected if Jesus were right by your side as you go about your daily routine. Picture him by your side as you flip the channel or do an Internet search. Let your attitude and your choices indicate that you are ready for his return. Be ready every second of the day to say, "I hope Jesus comes right now."

> **Make your life a place where you would feel proud to welcome Jesus.**

Live your life ready! Make every moment of your life be a welcome sight in the eyes of God. He will be back here before you know it.

Go therefore and make disciples of all the nations.

MATTHEW 28:19 NKJV

Tell Everyone

If you had the greatest news in the world, you would want to tell everyone. If someone you loved died and then came back to life, you would tell everyone about it. You wouldn't keep that kind of story to yourself. A story like that would make front-page news; it would get television news coverage for days.

Jesus died on a cross as payment for every person's offenses, and he came back to life three days later. After Jesus died and then came back to life, he asked his followers to tell everyone in every nation about God. The way to reach a nation is one person at a time. There are people all around you who have heard of God but don't know him personally.

You can tell people about God by sharing what you know about him. Offer to point out verses in the Bible that explain who God is. Talk to them about how much God loves every individual. To help them understand why knowing God is so important, you could describe what your life was like before you discovered God's love and

> There are people all around you who have heard of God but don't know him personally.

how it is now that you have experienced his love. Be willing to ask them to make a decision to believe in God and allow him to lead their life. Just like the disciples, you can do your part to make sure everyone everywhere has heard the great news about God and his love.

Reaching the nation with God's love can start with your own house, your own street, and your own school. Tell someone near you about God's love and how it changed your life.

LORD, every morning you hear my voice. Every morning, I tell you what I need, and I wait for your answer.

PSALM 5:3 NCV

Spend Time with God

No doubt you have a busy life. School, friends, extracurricular activities, youth group, or maybe even an after-school job keeps you hopping from the time you wake up until the time you go to bed. Are you carving out any time for God each day? All that activity places a burden on you—a burden that grows a little heavier each day if you aren't careful. God wants to bear that burden for you, to release you to a life of freedom. That means giving your cares and burdens to God every day.

Starting your day by spending time with God sets a stadard for your day. God becomes your first priority. Choose a quiet place to spend time with God. Some things you can choose to do during your time with God might include journaling, reading your Bible, and praying. Ask God to lead you in how or what you should do during your time with him. You might find that having a routine is comforting, or you may enjoy doing something different every time you meet with him.

> **Starting your day by spending time with God sets a standard for your day.**

Perhaps you might enjoy alternating days where one day you simply sit quietly and ask God to fill your mind and the next day you actively pursue the truth God has for you.

Meeting with God at the beginning of your day will give you the chance to tell him about your hopes. It will give you some time to consider how you will serve others and God that day. You can share your needs and cares with him instead of carrying them like a heavy load all day.

Set your alarm clock for fifteen minutes earlier in the morning so you make God first in your life. Talk to God about your day before it begins.

You, O God, have tested us; You have refined us as silver is refined.

PSALM 66:10 NKJV

You Will Be Tested

You may have taken the ACT or the SAT, but have you taken the GTYF? That stands for God Testing Your Faith. Your academic tests are important—they often determine what's in your future next year. God's testing may prepare you for the rest of your life. Jesus said that you would have trials and sorrows on earth, but that you can take heart—he has overcome the world. God tests you to examine your heart and make sure he has first place in your life. His kind of testing produces spiritual strength and growth.

A silversmith applies just the right amount of heat to silver to burn off the impurities. What remains is pure silver. God applies just the right amount of testing in your life to help you identify and get rid of things in your life that might compromise your character or your relationship with him.

Here is one way God might test you. You might find yourself in a situation where telling a lie is just as easy as telling the truth. By telling the truth, even when you are sure no one would know the difference if you lied, you strengthen

> **God tests you to help you identify weaknesses in your life and to make you stronger.**

your character. Another test might involve other people in your life. There may be a person in your life that you don't get along with, and God may be using that person to test your commitment to love others as God loves you. God tests you to help you identify weaknesses in your life and to make you stronger.

your character. Another test might involve other people in your life. There may be a person in your life that you don't get along with, and God may be using that person to test your commitment to love others as God loves you. God tests you to help you identify weaknesses in your life and to make you stronger.

Testing is an opportunity for you to grow in your relationship with God. When you are tested, ask God to show you what he wants you to learn.

Wherever your treasure is, there your heart and thoughts will also be.

MATTHEW 6:21 NLT

Your Treasure Defines Your Heart

Have you thought about what you treasure the most? It could be chatting with friends on-line, shopping, or skateboarding. You will protect whatever you treasure the most. For instance, if you treasure time with your friends, you will arrange your schedule so that you can spend the most time possible with them. Matthew 6:21 states a simple yet life-changing truth. What you treasure or love the most will control your thoughts and your heart. Treasuring something good is okay, but even too much of a good thing can be bad if it interferes with your relationships with others or your relationship with God. For example, serving others is good, but if you schedule so many service projects that you never see your family, serving may end up being a bad thing.

Whatever is most important in life will ultimately take priority in your thoughts. From your thoughts and your heart come your decisions, your interactions with others, and your relationship with God, so it's critical to make sure you know what you treasure. Not all treasure is good. For example, some people treasure pornography, alcohol, drugs, or sex. Treasuring any of these is dangerous to your mental, spiritual, and physical health.

> From your thoughts and your heart come your decisions, your interactions with others, and your relationship with God.

Take a deliberate inventory of what you think about during the day, and then decide what gets to hold a place in your heart and what does not. What you treasure will define who you are, so choose your treasure wisely.

Life is rich with good things to treasure like family, friends and fun stuff to do. Choose a balanced blend of these treasures that will enrich your life.

Your word is a lamp to my feet and a light to my path.

PSALM 119:105 NKJV

Lighted Way

On the Mammoth Cave tour, there is a spot where the guide turns off all the lights. It is so dark that you can't see your hand right in front of your face. Then the tour guide lights one match. It is amazing how one tiny bit of light can penetrate even the darkest place.

The Bible can do the same for you. The Bible will light the way as you go along in life. When a crisis comes along, you can go to the Bible to find the way to handle it. Jonah's crisis occurred when he disobeyed God. As a result he was swallowed by a whale. Reading Jonah's story can shed some light on what to do when things go bad. The Bible can direct you in dealing with the gray days that life brings. If you begin to doubt God, you can read about Peter, who struggled with doubt on more than one occasion. Even though he spent three years with Jesus, he had trouble believing all he

> **The Bible is filled with real stories about real people who lived real lives.**

had seen and heard about the power of God. Peter's story will bring light to your life and push out the darkness that doubt brings.

The Bible is like the match in the cave. One verse can pierce the darkness. The Bible is filled with real stories about real people who lived real lives. They had to deal with parents and friends and betrayal and confusion just as you do. God provided direction, guidance, and comfort to them then, as he does to you now.

If you aren't already systematically reading the Bible every day, start with Proverbs. Read a chapter of Proverbs every day. There are thirty-one chapters, so within a month you will have finished the book.

The person who trusts in the LORD will be blessed. The LORD will show him that he can be trusted.

JEREMIAH 17:7 NCV

You Can Trust Him

As you know, it takes a while to build trust in any relationship. Think about your best friends. You didn't just decide to trust one another; you trust each other because you know one another to be trustworthy. And if a friend ever betrays your trust, you know how long it takes to build back that trust.

You have lots of reasons to trust God. Here's a list of the top ten: (10) he is the Creator of the universe; (9) he never changes—never; (8) he knew you even before you were born; (7) he has been around a long time, is not going any-where, and is everlasting; (6) he knows how many hairs are on your head; (5) he has a plan for your life that is beyond your wildest dreams; (4) he hears your prayers; (3) he can divide an ocean in two; (2) his love for you knows no limits; and (1) he loves you so much that he allowed his only Son to die as payment for your pardon. These are just a few exam-ples from the Bible of God's strength, power, knowledge, longevity, and love for you.

The stresses and challenges of everyday life can make you lose sight of God's trustworthiness. You can't always see evidence of God's faithful-ness. But to trust a person means you continue to trust even in the absence of direct evidence. Do you want to strengthen your trust in God? Remind yourself of the things you know to be true about his faithfulness.

> **The stresses and challenges of everyday life can make you lose sight of God's trustworthiness.**

Trust God with something you have never given to him before—perhaps a request, a dream, or a problem you didn't think he could handle. Give it to God. You can trust him.

A thief comes to steal and kill and destroy, but I came to give life—life in all its fullness.

JOHN 10:10 NCV

Satan Is a Bad Guy

Jesus is the Good Shepherd. A shepherd protects his sheep from predators somewhat like a police officer protects innocent people from the bad guys. A shepherd stays with his sheep, guarding them from harm through the night and making sure they don't stray during the day.

Satan is a bad guy. He, like a wolf, is after the sheep. He is described in John 10:10 as a thief and a murderer. Satan is real, and he has a mission. He wants to ruin you. He wants to take away all the good in your life. He is in charge of evil. There is nothing good about him. The Bible says he can even appear to be an angel of light or appear to be good, but it is just a trick. You've probably noticed how things that aren't that good for you can seem mighty enticing. Satan is a master at that trick. His whole goal is to hurt people any way he can. But there's no reason to be afraid of Satan.

> Satan can't win; he can only irritate, trick, and entice you to do something wrong.

The Bible is clear that Satan is real and has some power, but his power is nothing compared to God's power. God is the One in control. Satan can't win; he can only irritate, trick, and entice you to do something wrong. He specializes in making people feel guilt, unworthiness, and complacency. You need to be aware that he exists, but you also need to be aware that the Good Shepherd protects you from Satan. Jesus desires to fill your life with goodness and joy.

There are two main errors with regard to Satan: taking him too lightly (or not believing in him at all) or taking him too seriously. Understand that Satan is real, but his power is nothing compared to the power of God.

A child has been born to us; God has given a son to us. He will be responsible for leading the people. His name will be Wonderful Counselor, Powerful God, Father Who Lives Forever, Prince of Peace.

ISAIAH 9:6 NCV

God's Son

Isaiah had the privilege and the burden of foretelling the birth, life, death, and resurrection of Jesus. His prophecy stands as one of the most significant predictions in the Bible. In a time of great suffering and darkness, he foretold of a King who would save the world. Isaiah identifies this child as the Son of God and as the leader of God's people. Isaiah's lists of names for the Son of God are a description of Jesus.

The word *wonderful* in Hebrew is *pele*, which means "extraordinary, hard to understand." The birth of Jesus certainly fit that description. No one could explain how a virgin could become pregnant and have a child. And the way Jesus healed people and provided for their deepest needs was nothing short of extraordinary. The Hebrew word for *counselor* is *ya' ats*, which means "to purpose, devise, and plan." Jesus came to fulfill God's plan. His purpose in life was to be the living sacrifice for all sin. The Hebrew word for *sin* is *gibbowr*, which means "strong, brave champion." Only the strongest and mightiest man could endure the sadness of being abandoned by friends and the shame of being falsely accused of a crime.

> The word *wonderful* in Hebrew is *pele*, *which* means "extraordinary, hard to understand." The birth of Jesus certainly fit that description.

Isaiah's prophecy came true when Jesus was born. The prophecy is evidence of God's divine plan for your life. It is the record of his love for you. It is proof that the Bible can be trusted.

Jesus was God in human form. He died on a cross for your sins and conquered death by coming back to life and returning to heaven.

Do you truly believe that Jesus was God's Son and that he lived, died, and rose again for your sake? If so, what do you plan to do about it?

I am the vine, and you are the branches. If any remain in me and I remain in them, they produce much fruit. But without me they can do nothing.

JOHN 15:5 NCV

A Relationship with Jesus

In the Old Testament, grapes were a symbol of fruitfulness or abundance accomplished when God's people followed him wholeheartedly. Jesus used the familiar Old Testament analogy in John 15:5. He told his followers that he wanted them to have abundance in all aspects of life. He wanted them to be fruitful by telling lots of other people about God.

On a grapevine, if the branch is connected to the vine, it can get all the water and nutrients it needs to produce huge clumps of big fat grapes. If the branch is broken off from the vine, any grapes on the branch spoil and go bad. The branch itself will wither and die if it is not a part of the vine. A grapevine paints a serious picture about how important it is for you to stay connected to Jesus.

To get to know someone and stay connected to that person, you have to spend time with him. The same is true about God. When you read the Bible, you will read the written form of God's words and thoughts. When you pray, you are talking to God. When you worship, you are honoring God and acknowledging how great and holy he is. All of this binds your heart to God. The only time a branch can live and produce fruit is when it is connected to the vine, when it is part of the vine. The same is true for you. When you are connected to God, your life will produce fruit.

> A grapevine paints a serious picture about how important it is for you to stay connected to Jesus.

Are you trying to live a good life in your own strength? If so, you're headed for total burnout. Connect to the Vine, Jesus. There you will receive strength for the life God has called you to.

Put all evil things out of your life: sexual sinning, doing evil, letting evil thoughts control you, wanting things that are evil, and greed.

COLOSSIANS 3:5 NCV

Get Rid of the Bad Stuff

Paul never met the believers in Colossae, a city in Asia Minor, but he wrote to them out of concern. A contingent of believers had introduced ideas into the church that weren't from God. The intent of Paul's letter was to set the believers straight, to clarify the truth, and to help them rid themselves of anything that contaminated the truth.

His letter focused on how Christians should live. Paul packed Colossians 3:5 with advice on several areas of Christian living. He addressed sexual impurity, emotions, human longings, and greed. Paul's point was this: in order for believers to live differently from everyone else, they had to identify sin in their own lives and get rid of it.

Paul's point is timeless. Evil, greed, immoral sexual thoughts, and other bad stuff will invade your day, too. The world you live in has become more accepting of things that are in direct opposition to what the Bible says is good, right, and true. You will have the opportunity to share your faith just by the choices you make about the clothing you wear, the words you use, the lyrics you listen to, the magazines you read, and more. Others will look

> **Take any decision you are unsure of to God for clarification.**

to your decisions to try to figure out what is right and what is wrong. Make sure your decisions don't introduce what Paul called "false doctrine." Take any decision you are unsure of to God for clarification. Live your life in a way that indulges in the love of God rather than evil.

Your life reflects what you believe in. Create a "scum box" and toss anything into it that might hinder your relationship with God. Empty your scum box into the trash often.

Do to others what you want them to do to you. This is the meaning of the law of Moses and the teaching of the prophets.

MATTHEW 7:12 NCV

Good Rule for You

You're almost to the passenger door of your friend's car when a voice rings out behind you: "Shotgun!" Talk about a moment of decision. Do you open the door and get in the front—after all, you've got the other guy boxed out—or do you follow the unwritten rule of car passengers every-where? The one who calls shotgun rides shotgun. The one who's too slow sits in the back with the discarded fast-food wrappers and the driver's gym bag, where you can't quite hear the conversation between the driver and the front-seat passenger.

The real problem, of course, is the whole tradition of calling shotgun. It's the exact opposite of the golden rule: "Do unto others what you want them to do to you." It allows a person to put himself or herself first with no more justification than the fact that he or she was thinking about sitting in the front seat when everybody else was thinking about something else.

The injustice you feel when somebody else calls shotgun and expects you to get in the backseat illustrates the wisdom of the golden rule. A moral code in which selfishness is the surest way to be rewarded (the reward of the front seat, for instance) is going to lead to resentment and anger. But if you treat others the way you would want to be treated, you contribute to the greater peace and harmony. You discover that front seat and backseat don't matter nearly as much as getting there together.

> The injustice you feel when somebody else calls shotgun and expects you to get in the backseat illustrates the wisdom of the golden rule.

Is there some area of your life where your unfair insistence on getting your way has spoiled things for another person — or maybe for yourself? Try treating that person the way you would have liked to be treated.

You are tempted in the same way that everyone else is tempted. But God can be trusted not to let you be tempted too much, and he will show you how to escape from your temptations.

1 Corinthians 10:13 CEV

Forget about the wrong things people do to you, and do not try to get even. Love your neighbor as you love yourself. I am the LORD.

LEVITICUS 19:18 NCV

Revenge

When somebody hurts you, the natural thing is to want to hurt that person back. You want payback. You want vigilante justice. You want to be Neo from *The Matrix*, striking a blow for the cause of justice—or at least for the cause of your own hurt feelings.

There's just one problem with getting even: how do you know when you're even? If someone owes you money, it's easy enough to figure out how to settle accounts. But when a person has caused you harm or gotten in your face or cost you self-respect, how does that account get settled? Hurting another person doesn't heal your hurt or restore your self-respect. Plotting revenge and holding a grudge won't ease your pain; in fact, they keep the wound open so it cannot heal.

Healing and peace come only through forgiveness. Has a friend turned her back on you for a more popular friend? Let it go. Has a teacher embarrassed you in front of the class? Let it slide. It's not easy, of course. It's not the "natural" thing to do. How do you even begin to do such a thing? By deciding

> **There's just one problem with getting even: how do you know when you're even?**

to love others as much as you love yourself. The people who hurt you can be messed up and confused, just like you are sometimes. That doesn't mean it's okay for them to hurt you; it just means it's up to you to keep their junk from spilling into your life. And you do that by forgiving.

Forgiveness isn't about rolling over and taking somebody else's abuse. It's about taking control of your own situation. Whom do you need to forgive in order to set yourself free?

Let no one despise your youth, but be an example to the believers in word, in conduct, in love, in spirit, in faith, in purity.

1 TIMOTHY 4:12 NKJV

Be the Example

"Kids these days!" You can be sure adults pay attention to the way young people conduct themselves, even if it's just to shake their heads and mutter that things ain't like they used to be. The Bible tells you not to let anyone despise your youth. And unfortunately, there are plenty of old grouches out there who do despise youth. But you have the ability to silence them. The way you convince the watching world that your generation isn't a lost cause is by living a godly life and by setting an example through the words you say and the way you conduct yourself in love and purity.

You're not too young to be a spiritual leader. You can set the tone in your interactions. It doesn't matter what your age is. You have to be eighteen to vote, thirty to run for the Senate, thirty-five to be elected president of the United States. But you can be a spiritual leader now by showing God at work in your life. If you are exhibiting the fruits of the Spirit, people will respect you. And if they don't respect you, that's their problem, not yours.

Adults don't have a monopoly on mature spirituality. As a matter of fact, you have one advantage over adults in that department: you're still too young to be set in your ways. There is a freshness to your spirituality that can be a real encouragement and challenge to the grownups around you. Jesus

> **If you are exhibiting the fruits of the Spirit, people will respect you.**

taught his followers to come to him like little children. You're not a kid anymore, but you may find it easier than most adults to remember what childlike faith is like. So go ahead. Be an example.

Are you tired of hearing how your generation is going to the dogs? Prove your critics wrong by setting an example of godliness.

I trust in God. I will not be afraid. What can people do to me?

PSALM 56:11 NCV

Fearless

Fourteen-year-old competitive surfer Bethany Hamilton was featured on a program called *Fearless*. The program is about people who push the limits in outdoor sports. A shark attacked Bethany while she was surfing. Her left arm had to be amputated just below the shoulder. A few months after her recovery, she went back in the water and placed fifth in the National Surfing Championship. In later interviews,

Bethany credited Jesus for her survival and her witness.

Nothing and no one can take you away from God. Bethany knows this intimately. Throughout the unbeliev-able horror of being attacked by a shark, she was not alone. God was

> God may not remove the circumstance or the fear, but he will be with you through it.

with her. God promises to be with you through every cir-cumstance. God may not remove the circumstance or the fear, but he will be with you through it. When you are afraid, remember to trust God. Trust him because of who he is.

It takes a lot more than courage to get back in the water if you have been bitten by a shark. For Bethany, her strength comes from her trust in God. There may be all kinds of bad things swimming around in your life. It may seem like dan-ger and disaster are circling all around you, ready to attack. Trust God to be with you. God is stronger than anyone or anything that might hurt you. You don't have to live in fear.

God is bigger than any problem or person who might threat-en you or the great life God has planned for you. You can live life without fear by putting your trust in God.

How can a young person live a pure life? By obeying your word.

PSALM 119:9 NCV

Purity

The potter's wheel is spinning. You feel the pot begin to take shape between your thumb and fingers, just as your art teacher said it would. The lump of formless clay is starting to look like something useful and beautiful. The soft smoothness of the clay feels good to your fingers. But then something hard brushes against your thumb. A split second later, on the next rotation, you feel it again, a little more solid, and then again. Before you realize what has happened, a pebble imbedded in the clay has ripped through the wall of your pot and left it a crumpled mess.

Impurity imbedded in your life can have a similar effect.

To keep your heart and mind clean means that you make a concentrated effort to avoid dwelling on sexual, violent, or evil thoughts. Purity means making a commitment to refrain from having sex until you are married. It means accepting responsibility for checking television shows, videos, and

> **Reading the Bible daily will trigger good choices about the things you do, the things you watch, and the things you listen to.**

music in plenty of time to make a clear choice before exposing yourself. Purity is a continuing, daily process.

And it's not just a matter of keeping bad things out. Purity is also about filling your heart and mind with good things. Reading the Bible daily will trigger good choices about the things you do, the things you watch, and the things you listen to. This is how you can succeed at living a life of purity. You are being shaped into something useful and beautiful. Don't let impurity spoil it.

Examine what is in your bedroom. Are there CDs, magazines, books, video games, or DVDs that don't reflect God's idea of clean living? Maybe it is time to clean your room in a new way.

The command says, "Honor your father and mother." This is the first command that has a promise with it—"Then everything will be well with you, and you will have a long life on the earth."

EPHESIANS 6:2–3 NCV

Honor Your Father and Mother

Sometimes it seems as if your parents can't possibly remember what it's like to be a teenager. The restrictions they put on you, the expectations they have—do they have any idea what it's like to have somebody telling you what to do all the time? A lot of things have changed since your parents were your age. And, yes, it's possible that they have forgotten a few things about what it's like to be a teen. But they may not be as out of touch as you think.

Your parents have lived through many of the experiences you're struggling through now. They may not have had mobile phones and instant messaging when they were growing up, but they did have final exams

> **Your parents make mistakes. Everybody does.**

and heartaches and all the exhilaration and insecurity of becoming an adult. What looks to you like an effort to control every aspect of your life may actually be your parents' desire to save you from having to learn things the hard way — maybe the way they had to learn themselves.

Your parents make mistakes. Everybody does. But your relationship with them will go a lot more smoothly if you remember that they want what's best for you, even if you're not sure they're going about it the right way. Honoring your parents doesn't mean agreeing with them all the time, but it does mean respecting their authority and trusting that their motives are good.

What is a trouble spot between you and your parents? Initiate a calm, loving conversation on this subject; tell your parents that you trust them, and ask them to help you understand their side of the issue. Who knows? Maybe your respectful approach will lead to a compromise.

Remind them to be subject to rulers and authorities, to obey, to be ready for every good work, to speak evil of no one, to be peaceable, gentle, showing all humility to all men.

TITUS 3:1–2 NKJV

Get Along

The Christians on the island of Crete faced an intense situation with the Roman government. The government ruled with force, especially when it came to groups they considered turbulent and noncompliant. Paul told them to maximize the qualities they saw in the life of Jesus.

Your life is changing so fast in many ways. You are expected to act like a grownup, but you aren't necessarily given the chance to take responsibility for yourself. You feel like you are ready to drive to a concert in the next town, but your parents say it is too far for someone your age to drive. It's a crazy time as your mom and dad give the job of parenting their last-ditch effort to prepare you for the real world. At the same time, your parents are acting weird because they feel they are losing you.

As a Christian teenager, you may be held to a higher standard than teens who don't claim any particular positive belief system. Paul had some advice. Respecting authority God has placed over you and doing your best to get along with others will save you a lot of hassle. Paul said to firmly apply God's standards to your life. Your love, kindness, and compliance will stand out as evidence of your

> **Your love, kindness, and compliance will stand out as evidence of your maturity and as a witness to your faith.**

maturity and as a witness to your faith. Doing this will smooth out your relationship with the people whom God has chosen to guide and direct you.

Rebelliously uphold the standards of God. Take kindness and respect for authority seriously. Surprise the people who oversee your life with radical compliance and respect.

I give you a new command: Love each other. You must love each other as I have loved you.

JOHN 13:34 NCV

Love One Another

Have you ever found yourself in a situation where two different people are friends with you, but they can't stand each other? It stresses you out. You wish each person could see what you see in the other. You wish they would be friends just for your sake, if for no other reason.

Jesus said, "Love each other as I have loved you." He might have said, "See one another as I have seen you." God loves you. And don't forget, he also loves that person you can't stand the sight of. Think about what that means. When

God looks at that person, he sees past all those things that drive you crazy. God loves that person in spite of his or her habit of smacking gum or constant whining or the tendency to say mean things about you behind your back. And it grieves God when you choose to see only the shortcomings in another person.

> God loves you. And don't forget, he also loves that person you can't stand the sight of.

"Love one another as I have loved you." That person isn't the only one who has shortcomings. God looks past some faults in you, too, when he looks at you. What would happen if God judged you as harshly as you judge other people? You've heard people say, "Any friend of so-and-so's is a friend of mine." That's a good policy to adopt with people who are loved by the same God who loves you: "Anybody loved by God is loved by me." That covers everybody.

There are probably people in your life toward whom you aren't very loving. It's time to start seeing them as people whom God loves. God sees past your failings. Why can't you see past theirs?

Immediately the father of the child cried out and said with tears, "Lord, I believe; help my unbelief!"

MARK 9:24 NKJV

Just Believe

A boy was possessed by a demon that caused him to have seizures and hurt himself physically. The father of the boy had tried for years to find help for his son. Ready to give up hope, he brought the boy to Jesus and begged him to do anything he could to help. Jesus replied that everything is possible for someone who believes. At this point the father asked Jesus to help his unbelief. Most people, at some moment in life, find themselves saying just what this father said: "I want to believe; help me believe."

Reading the Bible, going to church, and praying are merely activities until you come to a point in your life where you can't deny that God is working in your life and that God loves you no matter what. There will be times when you want to believe, but the situation you are in will indicate no hope is left. When

> **Most people, at some moment in life, find themselves saying just what this father said: "I want to believe; help me believe."**

you're up against that proverbial wall, keep your mind and your heart fixed on the power of belief. Remember the father's prayer to Jesus, and ask God to help you.

Cry out to God by journaling, praying, or writing a song about how you feel. Tell him you want to believe. God will provide the faith you need. Believing in God means going beyond what you think you know or what you think you see. Believing means saying God is right and God is good even when the circumstance you are in is not. Faith is believing even when the details of your life say give it up.

⌐⫯⫯⊙

Your doubt is not a weakness; it is a desire for more of what God has already shown you. God always has more faith to give you.

Long ago the LORD said to Israel: "I have loved you, my people, with an everlasting love. With unfailing love I have drawn you to myself."

JEREMIAH 31:3 NLT

I Will Love You Forever

When God's chosen people turned away from him, God sent Jeremiah as a prophet or messenger. God's people had forgotten and neglected God's love. Through Jeremiah, God faithfully promised to restore his people once they turned their affection and attention back toward him.

God placed in your heart a desire for pure, everlasting love that only he can fill. The love of a good mom and dad is a tiny sample of the nurturing love of God the Father. When you meet and marry Mr. or Miss Right, their love will give you a glimpse of the intimate love of God. The love you feel for others is a taste of how God feels about you. But none of these come close to the extent of God's love for you. Even when you turn away from God, his everlasting love draws you back to him.

Falling in love can be an intense experience, especially in the beginning. You can be swept away in the wonderful emotions that fill your heart. God is constantly calling you back to the moment you first realized his love for you. God's love, like his character, is unchangeable. He

> When you meet and marry Mr. or Miss Right, their love will give you a glimpse of the intimate love of God.

can't love you any more or any less than he has before; his love for you is perfect and complete. God draws you to himself with an everlasting love that will never die.

God's love is the love you have been looking for. Turn to him to fulfill your heart's desire for true love. Allow yourself to fall in love with God.

Jesus said to His disciples, "If anyone desires to come after Me, let him deny himself, and take up his cross, and follow Me."

MATTHEW 16:24 NKJV

Follow Me

As a kid you probably played follow the leader. One person gets to lead and everyone else has to do exactly what the leader does. Jesus is the leader, and you are to follow him. But doing exactly what Jesus would do won't be as easy as the child's game you played.

Matthew recorded a few ways that Jesus said to follow him. The first way to follow him is to deny yourself. In other words, allow Jesus to be the boss of your life instead of you being the boss. The second way to follow Jesus is to take up your cross, which is a strange way of saying don't avoid the tough stuff in your life. Bring it to Jesus. You will get stronger as you deal with the challenges in life. Do you have schedule conflicts? Peer pressures? Unexpected obstacles? Bring them all to Jesus. He won't make your problems disappear, but he'll give you the strength to keep going. If you are fol-

> **You will learn and grow spiritually as you imitate the character of Jesus.**

lowing him, you will be right where he wants you to be. You will be available to use the talents he has given you to honor him. You will learn and grow spiritually as you imitate the character of Jesus. You will be right where he can use you and bless you the most.

No one is forced to follow Jesus; you have to make your own decision to follow him. Following Jesus means constantly acknowledging him as the leader, the teacher, and the guide of your life. It may not always be easy to follow Jesus, but you will never find a better leader.

You can lead your own life or you can follow Jesus. There can only be one leader. Let God lead; his sense of direction is flawless.

"Now Moses, in the law, commanded us that such should be stoned. But what do You say?" This they said, testing Him, that they might have something of which to accuse Him. But Jesus stooped down and wrote on the ground with His finger, as though He did not hear. So when they continued asking Him, He raised Himself up and said to them, "He who is without sin among you, let him throw a stone at her first."

JOHN 8:5–7 NKJV

Offer Someone Forgiveness

Jesus found himself in a tricky situation. A woman was caught breaking the law. According to the law at that time, the punishment was death by stoning. A crowd of men stood around with rocks in their hands, waiting to throw them at the woman. Jesus didn't have a rock. Here is the tricky part—this was a setup, not for the woman, but for Jesus. If Jesus picked up a rock and helped stone the woman to death, he would prove he was just like everyone else. If Jesus didn't throw rocks at her, he would be in trouble for not following the law.

Jesus came up with an alternative and taught two important lessons in this one situation. By asking for anyone free of sin to throw the first stone, he pointed out that no one is perfect. As the mob surveyed their lives, they realized they had sinned at one time or another.

> Love and forgive other people when they mess up.

Eventually everyone dropped their rocks and left. Then Jesus talked to the woman. Jesus offered her forgiveness.

The same two lessons apply to you today. You have the opportunity to treat people better than they deserve when they get caught doing something wrong. Love and forgive other people when they mess up. Jesus is the role model for doing what is right.

You can offer forgiveness instead of judgment; the choice is up to you. Try to see every situation from the other person's perspective, and remember, no one is perfect.

> Seek first his kingdom and his righteousness, and all these things will be added to you.

MATTHEW 6:33 NASB

First Things First

God has structured the world such that if you focus your attention on the things that really matter, you also get the good things that don't matter as much. On the other hand, if you focus on the not-so-important things, you miss out on the important things, and you might not even get the less-important things you were shooting for.

Think of it this way: say, instead of actually learning the material for your biology test, you cram the night before to get a decent grade. Maybe you do make a decent grade, but the next test builds on the last one, and it's even harder to make a decent grade on that one than on the first. The more you focus on your grade, the harder it will be to make the grade . . . and you probably will not have learned very much. On the other hand, if you had been focusing from the start on what really matters—on learning biology—you would

> The more you focus on your grade, the harder it will be to make the grade . . . and you probably will not have learned very much.

have found good grades to be a natural by-product of your knowledge. You would enjoy biology *and* enjoy the good grades you had earned as a reward for your hard work.

That's how all of life works, not just biology class. As you focus on the things of God, you will find that the other good things you've been seeking—friendship, love, the respect of your peers, security, self-esteem—will begin to fall into place.

What have you been seeking before the kingdom of God? Give that over to God; let him give you those things in his way—as a by-product of a life lived for him.

Let no one despise
your youth, but be an
example to the believers
in word, in conduct, in
love, in spirit, in faith,
in purity.

1 TIMOTHY 4:12 NKJV

The Helper will teach you everything and will cause you to remember all that I told you. This Helper is the Holy Spirit whom the Father will send in my name.

JOHN 14:26 NCV

Someone Is There for You

Jesus promised the disciples that he would not leave them alone and abandoned once he was gone. He told them he would ask God to send a Helper to his disciples. Although they would not be able to physically see this Helper, called the Holy Spirit, they would be aware of the presence of the Holy Spirit. The Holy Spirit showed up just as Jesus had promised when the disciples were praying together. The Holy Spirit filled them with the energy and the abilities they needed to teach and preach about God with confidence.

The Greek word for *helper* is *parakletos*. It is "someone who is called to one's side or one's aid," "a counselor, an advocate, someone who pleads another's case before a judge." The Holy Spirit is continuing what Jesus started. Guidance, wis-

> **Guidance, wisdom, authority, protection, and comfort all come from the Holy Spirit to you.**

dom, authority, protection, and comfort all come from the Holy Spirit to you.

The Holy Spirit is the source of your ability to study and understand the Bible. The Holy Spirit is the comfort you receive from God when you walk through the difficult times in life. The Holy Spirit is that internal nudge you feel when you hesitate to do something you know God wants you to do. The Holy Spirit is the quiet voice inside that assures you and guides you when you commit to living according to God's design.

If you have not experienced the full capacity and momentum you desire for your spiritual life, ask God to reveal more about his Holy Spirit.

He is not here; he has risen from the dead.

LUKE 24:6 NCV

Jesus Is Alive

Several women who had followed Jesus during his ministry got up very early in the morning on the first day of the week and, carrying the spices that they had prepared, went to the place where he had been buried. When they got there, the large stone that covered his tomb had been moved to the side and the tomb was open. The women looked for Jesus's body, but it was gone. Jesus was no longer there. The women were frightened. Had someone stolen Jesus's body?

Jesus is alive. A majority of the religions in the world center on a divinity or a person who is no longer alive. Not only is Jesus alive, but he was raised from the dead. Jesus came to earth to save you from being permanently separated from God. If the story ended with Jesus's dying to save you, he

> Like any good relationship, your relationship with God will grow as you spend time with him.

would be just another dead god. But it doesn't end there. He came back to life. You have the ability to be in a relationship with the living God.

Instead of simply knowing God, you can know God personally. Think of God as you think of your best friend. A best friend is someone you can trust, someone whom you can share your hopes and dreams with. When you have questions or problems, a best friend is there to listen and to give you guidance. Your relationship with God is a special friendship. Like any good relationship, your relationship with God will grow as you spend time with him. Spending time with God is possible because he is alive.

Only living things grow. Keep your relationship with God alive. Water and feed it with prayer and Bible study.

Give all your worries to him, because he cares about you.

1 PETER 5:7 NCV

No Worries; God Cares

There will be times in life when you feel that no one cares and no one is listening. It can hit you in a crowd at school or standing next to your family at church. It isn't out of the question to feel lonely even when you are not alone. In those moments it is crucial to set your thoughts on what the Bible says rather than be drawn in by the emotion of loneliness.

Often it is worry that drives you to isolate yourself. Pulling away from God and from the people who could support you is a natural reaction to pain and difficulty. Paul addressed this type of situation in his letter to a group of very discouraged Christians. Those people were being threatened, beaten, imprisoned, and even killed for believing Jesus was the Son of God and the eternal King. They felt abandoned by God. Paul urged them not to submit to circumstance and emotion, but to remain confident in the truth they had heard and witnessed.

> You can safely hand over your worry to God and be absolutely confident he cares.

Paul went on to say that it is the enemy, Satan, who wants to destroy faith with worry and isolation. The truth is, God loves you. Any worry you have is a concern to him. You can safely hand over your worry to God and be absolutely confident he cares. Despite what the enemy would like you to believe, you are not alone. The worries that threaten to overwhelm you will never overwhelm God.

Lighten your load of worries by sharing them with the ones who love you. Start with the One who loves you most — God. Give him what is getting you down.

If my people, who are called by my name, are sorry for what they have done, if they pray and obey me and stop their evil ways, I will hear them from heaven. I will forgive their sin, and I will heal their land.

2 CHRONICLES 7:14 NCV

Humble Is the Way

Saying you're sorry isn't easy, whether you're apologizing to a friend you've blown off, or apologizing for a fender bender in your parents' car. But saying you're sorry—and more important, changing your ways when you've messed up—is key to any healthy relationship, including your relationship with God.

Sometimes you have to deal with people who refuse to forgive a wrong, no matter how much you apologize, or how much you have changed. But not God. God promises that when you say you're sorry and turn away from your wrong habits and actions, he forgives and brings healing to your life.

In 2 Chronicles 7, the people of God were celebrating the completion of the temple in Jerusalem. The ceremony commemorated God's gifts to his people and their gifts of obedience back to him. God's words to them were a review of how Solomon and his people had finally come to this place of stability after so many years of wandering and turmoil. It wasn't because of their own might or strength or wisdom or goodness; it was because they had learned to put their pride aside, ask for forgiveness when they messed up, and allow God to be God.

> No matter how often or how badly you've messed up, God hears you when you ask him to forgive you.

No matter how often or how badly you've messed up, God hears you when you ask him to forgive you. He never gives up on you. God's healing and forgiveness are yours for the asking. All you have to do is to put away your pride and ask.

What wrong habits or wrong actions do you need to confess and turn away from? Asking God for forgiveness is part of your obedience to him. Obedience to God clears the way for him to bless you.

Listen! I am coming soon! I will bring my reward with me, and I will repay each one of you for what you have done.

REVELATION 22:12 NCV

Jesus Will Be Back

Listen! Has he gotten your attention? In the closing chapter of the Bible, Jesus appeals to you with a sense of urgency to confirm your relationship with him. There will be a day when Jesus returns to abolish all your doubts and settle all accounts.

When he returns, you will clearly know a full account of your life. You will see times when you missed an opportunity to share God's love. You will also see the impact of the moments you shared God's love through your words or actions. You will know without a doubt the answers to all the things in the Bible and in life that might be unanswered now. Just think of how exciting that will be.

From the beginning of the Bible in Genesis, all the way to the book of Revelation, the story of God's love for you unfolds and is retold and reaffirmed. In the Old Testament, God reached out to the human race over and over again, offering a way for men and women to reach God. Each time God reached out, men and women fell short of the perfection

> **There will be a day when Jesus returns to abolish all your doubts and settle all accounts.**

required to be with God. But God made a way to reach out beyond your imperfection. He sent Jesus. Jesus made you perfect and beautiful before God. Until Jesus returns, the Holy Spirit will be your companion, and the Bible will be your guide to all God has planned for your life. Jesus is coming back, and you will be ready to enjoy his love and the rewards he has for you.

Give away all you know about the love of God, and you will receive a great prize in heaven. Your prize will be wrapped in the unending love of God.

If someone says, "I love God," and hates his brother, he is a liar; for he who does not love his brother whom he has seen, how can he love God whom he has not seen?

1 JOHN 4:20 NKJV

Love the One You Are With

You get your ability to love others from God. Your motivation to love others is grounded in the fact that God loved you first. When you were unlovely and unlovable, God still loved you. In your best moments and your worst, good or bad, self-centered or self-less, God loved you. God set a standard that calls you to love others without conditions.

The writer of 1 John 4:20 pointed out to his Christian brothers and sisters how easy it was to say they loved God, whom they do not see. In other words, it is easy to say you love God since you could not have to live with him in the flesh. It is much more challenging to love someone you can see, smell, touch, and hear. Your love may have to overcome body odor, bad breath, and loud, harsh words. The person you are trying to love may get in your

> Love should begin with the people you live with and the people you spend the most time with.

face and deny your love, but you are called to love unconditionally. Sometimes the unlovely are easier to love than your own friends and family.

Loving the people from a poor country or in a recovery facility may be easier than loving the people you live with. It is your mom, dad, sister, or brother who can really get on your nerves since you are with them so much. Love should begin with the people you live with and the people you spend the most time with. The Scripture is clear that your ability to love others is the true test of how serious you are about loving God.

His love is engraved on your hearts, as if to say "100 percent love." You are permanently marked to love others. With God's imprint on your heart, you can't help but love others.

Anyone who knows the right thing to do, but does not do it, is sinning.

What Is Sin?

A life lived for God's glory can't be passive. Just steering clear of the thou-shalt-nots doesn't make you godly. Obedience to God means pursuing the good things that God calls you to.

There are sins of commission and sins of omission. Sometimes it's easy to consider only the things you do that you know you shouldn't; but you need also to consider the things you don't do that you know you should. You are guilty of a sin of commission when you know something is

204   THE 100 MOST IMPORTANT BIBLE VERSES FOR TEENS

wrong but you do it anyway. You cheat on a test or lie to a parent or steal somebody's lunch money. Those sins frequently involve an active decision: *I think I'll spray-paint some graffiti on the side of a grocery store.* On the other hand, a sin of omission is one you commit by *not* doing something: you know the right thing to do, but

> **A sin of omission is one you commit by *not* doing something.**

you don't do it. You know it's right to help the needy, but you just don't get around to it. You know you should go visit your grandmother, but you've always got something else going on. Sins of omission are sneaky. They happen while you're thinking about something else. You don't wake up and say, "I think I'll neglect some duties today." No, you just go about your day, and then, after it's too late, you realize you haven't put first things first.

You've got a busy schedule. But that doesn't let you off the hook for obedience. If you know what to do and don't do it, it's as if you have actively chosen to do something you know to be wrong. A sin of omission is still a sin.

Just steering clear of wrong doesn't make you right. You know the right things to do: go do them. No excuses.

In all the work you are doing, work the best you can. Work as if you were doing it for the Lord, not for people.

COLOSSIANS 3:23 NCV

Whom Are You Working For?

Digging a ditch is hard, dull, repetitive work. You stick your shovel in the ground; you scoop up the dirt; you heave the dirt out of the hole. Over and over again. Digging for buried treasure, on the other hand, is a very different experience. It's just as hard and just as repetitive. The physical aspects of the job are more or less the same. The difference is the treasure hunter's attitude. The treasure hunter digs with a sense of purpose and a lot of hope. If all goes well, he'll have great riches when he's through digging. If all goes well for the ditchdigger, he'll have, well, a ditch.

Your attitude makes all the difference in how your work goes. And a key aspect of your attitude toward your work—whether it's schoolwork, household chores, or any other kind of work—is your sense of purpose. Paul pointed out that what-

> **Even dull, repetitive work is meaningful if you are doing it to please God.**

ever work you do, your boss, ultimately, is God. And that means your work is important. Even dull, repetitive work is meaningful if you are doing it to please God.

The whole world belongs to God. He is the God of all knowledge, and so your schoolwork matters to him. He created the home, and so he is pleased when you pull your weight around the house and contribute to a more peaceful home life. He is the God even of the workplace; so flip burgers to God's glory, if that's your job.

Think about all the roles you play: student, employee, son or daughter, sibling, for starters. Have you been working to please God in all of those roles?

Spend time with the wise and you will become wise, but the friends of fools will suffer.

PROVERBS 13:20 NCV

Walk with the Wise

How would you describe your friends? Where do your friends like to hang out? Is it the kind of place you would be okay taking a youth pastor to? What do your friends like to do? Do you spend time with friends who encourage you and help you be the best person you can be? That's what wise friends do for each other.

A wise person is described as understanding, someone who exercises good judgment. A wise person learns from his or her mistakes and avoids making them again. A wise friend is interested in what others have to say. A wise friend admits when he or she is wrong. A wise friend will help you avoid getting into trouble.

Making a decision to hang around unwise people has a consequence. The consequence is that eventually you will share in someone else's unwise decision and get into trouble—usually it is more trouble than you anticipated. Avoid spending too much time with friends who continually make mistakes. If you have a friend who seems to make poor choices, figure out a way to lead in the relationship instead of following. You can care for that friend by taking the lead in areas where he or she has messed up in the past. If your friend fails to follow your lead, consider spending less time together. Make an effort to spend the majority of your time with people who consistently do the right thing. Choose to be with people who are known for their smart choices.

> Make an effort to spend the majority of your time with people who consistently do the right thing.

Some of your friends may know a lot, but a wise friend is someone who takes knowledge and applies it to his or her life. Wise friends bring out the best in you.

Serve only the LORD your God. Respect him, keep his commands, and obey him. Serve him and be loyal to him.

DEUTERONOMY 13:4 NCV

No Substitute

The Israelites faced a bit of a challenge. All their neighbors were worshiping things they could see—the sun, the moon, statues, their rulers. You get the picture. The Israelites were supposed to worship a God they couldn't see. So every time they started feeling insecure about their relationship with God—which seemed to be all the time—they made idols for themselves or started worshiping the gods of their neighbors. They thought they needed something they could see.

Does that sound ridiculous? Primitive? Not so fast. You live in a culture that's full of false gods and idols. Movie stars. Brand names. Sports heroes. Success. Popularity. Think how many things in your life promise to give you what only God can give: acceptance, love,

> **You live in a culture that's full of false gods and idols.**

self-respect, security. Every time you put your trust in any of those things (even the good things) in place of God, you're doing what the Israelites did when they took up with their neighbors' gods. Idolatry isn't about carving idols out of stone or wood. It's about placing anything or anyone in the place where God belongs.

There's a God-shaped hole in your heart. God is perfectly willing to fill it. And only he can. Sure, there are lots of other things clamoring to be put in God's place. But all of them will leave you empty. It takes faith to believe in someone you cannot see. But nothing else can take his place.

Think about how you spend your time, your money, and your effort. Does what you do acknowledge that you worship God above everything else?

A person's body is only one thing, but it has many parts. Though there are many parts to a body, all those parts make only one body. Christ is like that also.

1 CORINTHIANS 12:12 NCV

Each One Has a Part

No doubt you've seen reruns of the old *Addams Family* television show. You'll remember Thing, the disembodied hand that rises up out of its box to write down a message or beckon a visitor into the parlor. Thing is funny, but also creepy in a cheesy, sixties, black-and-white sort of way, because everybody knows a hand can't live on its own. Without a body to be attached to, a hand quickly dies. There's no part of the human body, in fact, that's self-sufficient. As important as the heart is, it can't survive without the kidneys or the esophagus. It works the other way around, too. Even those parts of the body that seem unimportant or less than respectable play a vital role in the functioning of the whole system. Nobody would want to be a lower intestine, but you'd be in a world of hurt without it. Even one missing toe means serious balance problems for the whole body.

> **You need the body of Christ. And the body needs you.**

The church is the body of Christ, and every part of it is important. You may feel like a nobody. You may think you've got nothing to contribute to the life of the church. But you have a role to play, even if you're not sure what it is. And by the same token, nobody is so important that he or she can survive spiritually apart from the body. You need the body of Christ. And the body needs you.

You have a role to play in the church, even if you don't know exactly what it is. Don't be discouraged. And don't even think about going it alone if you're serious about your spiritual health.

Run from anything that stimulates youthful lust. Follow anything that makes you want to do right. Pursue faith and love and peace, and enjoy the companionship of those who call on the Lord with pure hearts.

2 Timothy 2:22 nlt

Run Away

You will eventually face a situation where your best option is to walk away. For example, if you are on a date and the physical contact increases toward a point where you know you are about to compromise the boundaries you feel God has shown you, stop. According to Paul, your best option is to stop and move the date to a place where there is no privacy.

Choose to do things that will help you uphold your commitment to God instead of challenging it. A date with a group of friends to meet for soft drinks might be a better choice than a date for just two people alone. Paul pointed out that having friends who love God and who are dedicated to his ways is key to keeping one's commitment to God. By hanging out with Christian friends, you are more likely to do things that support your standards.

By putting yourself in situations you know God approves of, with friends who love God, you will find that you enjoy life without stressing over stuff that tempts you. In addition, you set yourself up to be used by God in a positive way to influence the lives of others. Paul wanted Timothy to live right so that he would always be ready

> As you live out your commitment to God, people around you will be attracted to the goodness in your life.

to share God's love. As you live out your commitment to God, people around you will be attracted to the goodness in your life. You will be ready to share with them that the sweet life you and your friends enjoy comes from God.

When temptation comes your way, go a different direction. Choose a direction that will lead to good friends who are dedicated to helping you keep your commitment to God.

Do not worry about anything, but pray and ask God for everything you need, always giving thanks.

PHILIPPIANS 4:6 NCV

Don't Worry, Pray

Time spent worrying is a waste. An hour spent worrying whether so-and-so really likes you. Twenty minutes spent worrying whether you studied hard enough for your history test. Thirty minutes spent worrying if your best friend is mad at you. The solution to worry is prayer and thankfulness, which can restore joy to any situation.

God already knows your needs and your desires; in fact, he knows them better than you do. If you know and trust God, you will turn all your worries over to him. Your confidence in God will result in thankfulness for his abilities.

Your worries will be replaced by peace as you thank God for taking care of you. Pray, do what you can, give God your worries, and rest in the assurance that God can help you solve any problem you have, from dating and friendships to schoolwork. Resting in God's abilities is much better than stressing about things.

Knowing that God can handle anything, you will be able to thank him when things are good and when things are bad. Since he is always looking out for your best interests, you can be certain that God will show you the joy in the midst of the most difficult situation. Paul described it this way: God's peace, which is so unprecedented that it defies human understanding, will keep your heart and mind bound to Jesus. When you pray, you focus your heart and your mind on the endless capacity of God rather than on the strain of your circumstance. Your fears and concerns are replaced by the might of the God who hears your prayers.

> **You can be certain that God will show you the joy in the midst of the most difficult situation.**

You have a God who cares about every single thought, concern, and moment of your life. Turn your worries over to God rather than lugging them around yourself.

No one can see God, but Jesus Christ is exactly like him. He ranks higher than everything that has been made.

COLOSSIANS 1:15 NCV

You Know God

Jesus knew from an early age that he was different. He had an understanding of God that no other person had. This unique understanding was the mind of God contained inside him. This almost incomprehensible idea stated another way is this: Jesus was fully God and fully human all at once.

Paul hoped to help people gain an understanding of this matchless human named Jesus. Colossians 1 contains several verses of bite-size information to help people digest the concept of Jesus as fully God and fully human. The concept may take you a lifetime to grasp, and that is okay. Many adults still struggle with such a mind-boggling concept. Just remember that there is only one God.

Jesus was the living, breathing reality of God on earth. For you, this means two significant things. One, you can know God by knowing Jesus. Although much of who God is remains beyond human

> **Jesus was the living, breathing reality of God on earth.**

comprehension, the Bible gives you knowledge of God as you read about the life of Jesus. Two, Jesus experienced life as a human being. He was a baby, a child, a teenager, and an adult. Jesus was hungry, frustrated, happy, and sad. He experienced the loss of family and friends. Although he never gave in, Jesus was tempted by Satan, so he understands what it is like when you are tempted. He endured physical pain. Jesus knows what it is like to be human, which means he knows what it's like to be you.

God not only created humanity, but he experienced it firsthand. God knows what you are going through; allow him to be God in your life.

He was wounded for the wrong we did; he was crushed for the evil we did. The punishment, which made us well, was given to him, and we are healed because of his wounds.

ISAIAH 53:5 NCV

What Jesus Did

God often works in unexpected ways. What Isaiah was predicting didn't make sense from a human perspective. It sounded cruel and unjust. It did not seem possible that one person would take the punishment for what another person did wrong. There is no way injuring one person could heal another person. Isaiah's words finally made sense the day Jesus died on the cross nearly seven hundred years later.

Isaiah talked about a person who would come to lead and save people. In Isaiah's time, most leaders were strong individuals, physically, mentally, or both. The description in Isaiah 53:5 is of someone who was *beaten* and *crushed* — not the words you would typically associate with a leader, just the opposite, in fact. The key to understanding this verse is the realization that this leader would take the pain and suffering of others in order to spare them, in order to save them from having to endure it.

> **What Jesus did ensured that you will enjoy a permanent and unbreakable relationship with God.**

You are loved so much that God devised a plan that made it possible for Jesus to bear the pain and suffering that really belonged to you. Jesus took your place. His pain and his death made it possible for you to be healed. You are healed of the hurt that comes from being separated from God. As a result of his suffering, you can have a peace that comes from knowing you will never be separated from God. What Jesus did ensured that you will enjoy a permanent and unbreakable relationship with God.

God is a leader who is willing to replace your pain with joy. He loves you so much that he made sure you could be with him forever.

When you do things, do not let selfishness or pride be your guide. Instead, be humble and give more honor to others than to yourselves.

PHILIPPIANS 2:3 NCV

Others First

Paul was writing to the Christians in Philippi from a prison in Rome. Paul had started the church in Philippi on his second of three missionary journeys. He encouraged the Christians there to continue their good work. Paul told them to be interested in the lives of other people more than in their own lives. He encouraged them to think and act like Jesus. Jesus considered the needs of others more important than his own needs. Even though he was God in human form, he served others.

Jesus could have been and done anything he wanted to. He could have been a political success and risen to the position of earthly king. The possibilities for wealth or personal fame were endless. Instead he chose to spend time with people who were lost, lonely, sick, and hopeless. He used his power to heal and save others. He did ordinary things like attending a wedding or eating a meal with friends. In one of his most humble moments, he washed the dirty feet of his disciples so they might understand how important it was to serve others and remain humble.

> **Jesus never considered himself better than anyone else, even though he was.**

Jesus never considered himself better than anyone else, even though he was. His life was a phenomenal display of humility. Put others first by treating everyone the same. Take the initiative to put the best interest, of others first.

Putting others first goes against your very nature. In fact, in your own strength, you can't even do it—not on a consistent basis. If you're going to obey this command, you're going to have to turn it over to the One who succeeded in putting others first for a whole lifetime.

Go therefore and make disciples of all the nations.

MATTHEW 28:19 NKJV